GRANTS AND FUNDING

A GOVERNMENT GUIDE TO GRANTS

GRANTS AND FUNDING

Federal Student Loans
Tanya Shohov (Editor)
2004. ISBN: 1-59033-940-1

Grants: Introduction, Sources and Bibliography
Jean M. Fromm (Editor)
2006. ISBN: 1-59454-510-3

A Government Guide to Grants
Nathan E. Legaspi (Editor)
2010. ISBN: 978-1-60876-751-9

Fighting Fraud with Qui Tam and the False Claims Act
Ian M. Ortiz (Editor)
2010. ISBN: 978-1-61668-221-7

GRANTS AND FUNDING

A GOVERNMENT GUIDE TO GRANTS

NATHAN E. LEGASPI
EDITOR

Nova Science Publishers, Inc.
New York

Copyright © 2010 by Nova Science Publishers, Inc.

All rights reserved. No part of this book may be reproduced, stored in a retrieval system or transmitted in any form or by any means: electronic, electrostatic, magnetic, tape, mechanical photocopying, recording or otherwise without the written permission of the Publisher.

For permission to use material from this book please contact us:
Telephone 631-231-7269; Fax 631-231-8175
Web Site: http://www.novapublishers.com

NOTICE TO THE READER

The Publisher has taken reasonable care in the preparation of this book, but makes no expressed or implied warranty of any kind and assumes no responsibility for any errors or omissions. No liability is assumed for incidental or consequential damages in connection with or arising out of information contained in this book. The Publisher shall not be liable for any special, consequential, or exemplary damages resulting, in whole or in part, from the readers' use of, or reliance upon, this material. Any parts of this book based on government reports are so indicated and copyright is claimed for those parts to the extent applicable to compilations of such works.

Independent verification should be sought for any data, advice or recommendations contained in this book. In addition, no responsibility is assumed by the publisher for any injury and/or damage to persons or property arising from any methods, products, instructions, ideas or otherwise contained in this publication.

This publication is designed to provide accurate and authoritative information with regard to the subject matter covered herein. It is sold with the clear understanding that the Publisher is not engaged in rendering legal or any other professional services. If legal or any other expert assistance is required, the services of a competent person should be sought. FROM A DECLARATION OF PARTICIPANTS JOINTLY ADOPTED BY A COMMITTEE OF THE AMERICAN BAR ASSOCIATION AND A COMMITTEE OF PUBLISHERS.

LIBRARY OF CONGRESS CATALOGING-IN-PUBLICATION DATA

Available upon request.

ISBN : 978-1-60876-751-9

Published by Nova Science Publishers, Inc. ✦ New York

CONTENTS

Preface		vii
Chapter 1	Block Grants: Perspectives and Controversies *Robert Jay Dilger and Eugene Boyd*	1
Chapter 2	Grants Work in a Congressional Office *Merete F. Gerli*	27
Chapter 3	How to Develop and Write a Grant *Merete F. Gerli*	61
Chapter 4	Resources for Grant Seekers *Merete F. Gerli*	81
Chapter Sources		93
Index		95

PREFACE

This book provides an overview of the six grant types, provides criteria for defining a block grant and uses that criteria to provide a list of current block grants, examines competing perspectives concerning the use of block grants versus other grant mechanisms to achieve national goals, provides a brief historical overview of the role of block grants in American federalism, and examines recent changes to existing block grants and proposals to create new ones. The authors also describe key sources of information on government and private funding, and outlines eligibility for federal grants. Moreover, how to develop and write a grant proposal is also discussed in this book. In preparation for writing a proposal, the report first examines preliminary information gathering and preparation, developing ideas for the proposal, gathering community support, identifying funding resources, and seeking preliminary review of the proposal and support of relevant administrative officials. The second section covers the actual writing of the proposal, from outlining the project goals, to finally developing the proposal budget. This book consists of public documents which have been located, gathered, combined, reformatted, and enhanced with a subject index, selectively edited and bound to provide easy access.

Chapter 1 - Block grants are a form of grant-in-aid that the federal government uses to provide state and local governments a specified amount of funding to assist them in addressing broad purposes, such as community development, social services, public health, or law enforcement. The American Recovery and Reinvestment Act of 2009 (ARRA, P.L. 111-5), which became law on February 17, 2009, provided additional funding to a number of block grant programs, including an additional $5 billion for the Temporary Assistance to Needy Families (TANF) block grant, $3.2 billion for the newest block grant program, the Energy Efficiency and Conservation Block Grant, $2 billion for

Edward Byrne Memorial Justice Assistance Grants, $2 billion for the Child Care Development Block Grant, and $1 billion for the Community Development Block Grant Program.

Block grants advocates view block grants as a means to increase government efficiency and program effectiveness by redistributing power and accountability through decentralization and partial devolution of decision-making authority. Their critics view them as a means to undermine the achievement of national objectives and as a "backdoor" means to reduce government spending on domestic issues. They also claim that the decentralized nature of block grants make it difficult to measure block grant performance and to hold state and local government officials accountable for their decisions.

Block grants, which have been a part of the American federal system since 1966, are one of three general types of grants-in-aid programs: categorical grants, block grants and general revenue sharing. These grants differ along three dimensions: the range of federal control over who receives the grant, the range of recipient discretion concerning aided activities, and the type, number, detail, and scope of grant program conditions.

Categorical grants can be used only for a specifically aided program, usually are limited to narrowly defined activities, and legislation generally details the program's parameters and specifies the types of funded activities. There are four types of categorical grants: project categorical grants, formula-project categorical grants, formula categorical grants, and open-end reimbursement categorical grants.

Project categorical grants and general revenue sharing represent the ends of a continuum on the three dimensions differentiating grant types, with block grants being at the mid-point. However, there is some overlap among grant types in the middle of the continuum. For example, some block grants have characteristics normally associated with formula categorical grants. This overlap, and the variation in characteristics among block grants, helps to explain why there is some disagreement concerning precisely what is a block grant, and how many of them exist.

This chapter provides an overview of the six grant types, provides criteria for defining a block grant and uses that criteria to provide a list of current block grants, examines competing perspectives concerning the use of block grants versus other grant mechanisms to achieve national goals, provides a brief historical overview of the role of block grants in American federalism, and examines recent changes to existing block grants and proposals to create new ones.

Chapter 2 - Members of Congress receive frequent requests from grant seekers needing funds for projects in districts and states. The congressional office should first determine its priorities regarding the appropriate assistance to give constituents, from providing information on grants programs to active advocacy of projects. Congressional grants staff can best help grant seekers by first themselves gaining some understanding of the grants process.

Each office handles grants requests in its own way, depending upon the Member's legislative agenda and overall organization and workload. There may be a full-time grants specialist or several staff members under the supervision of a grants coordinator working solely in the area of grants and projects. In some offices, all grants requests are handled in the district or state office; in others, they are answered by the Washington, DC, staff.

To assist grant seekers applying for federal funds, congressional offices can develop working relationships with grants officers in federal and state departments and agencies. Because more than 90% of federal funds go to state and local governments that, in turn, manage federal grants and sub-award to applicants in their state, congressional staff need to identify their own state administering offices. For example, much of the current economic stimulus funding (see the website Recovery.gov at http://www.recovery) is being allocated through existing grants-in- aid programs.

To educate constituents, a congressional office may sometimes provide selected grant seekers information on funding opportunities; or may sponsor seminars on federal and private assistance. Because most funding resources are on the Internet, Member home pages can also link to grants sources such as the *Catalog of Federal Domestic Assistance* and *Grants.gov* so that constituents themselves can search for grants and funding opportunities. The CRS Web page, *Grants and Federal Domestic Assistance*, Merete F. Gerli (see sample at http://www.crs.gov/reference/ general/grants/member-grant.html), can be added to a Member's home page upon request, and is updated automatically on House and Senate servers. Another CRS Web page, *Grants, Business Opportunities, and Student Financial Aid*, by Mereti F. Gerli, at http://www.crs.gov/reference/general/WG02001.shtml, covers key CRS products.

Congressional staff can use CRS reports to learn about grants work and to provide information on government and private funding. In addition to the current report, these include CRS Report RS21 117, *Ethical Considerations in Assisting Constituents With Grant Requests Before Federal Agencies*, by Jack Maskell; CRS Report RL34012, *Resources for Grantseekers*, by Merete F. Gerli; and CRS Report RL32 159, *How to Develop and Write a Grant Proposal*, by Merete F. Gerli. CRS also offers reports on block grants and the appropriations process;

federal assistance for homeland security and terrorism preparedness; and federal programs on specific subjects and for specific groups, such as state and local governments, police and fire departments, libraries and museums, nonprofit organizations, small business, and other topics. An internal grants manual outlining office policies and procedures should be developed to help grants staff. With reductions in federal programs, grants specialists should also become familiar with other funding, such as private or corporate foundations, as alternatives or supplements to federal grants.

Chapter 3 - This chapter is intended for Members and staff assisting grant seekers in districts and states and covers writing proposals for both government and private foundations grants. In preparation for writing a proposal, the report first discusses preliminary information gathering and preparation, developing ideas for the proposal, gathering community support, identifying funding resources, and seeking preliminary review of the proposal and support of relevant administrative officials.

The second section of the report covers the actual writing of the proposal, from outlining of project goals, stating the purpose and objectives of the proposal, explaining the program methods to solve the stated problem, and how the results of the project will be evaluated, to long-term project planning, and, finally, developing the proposal budget.

The last section of the report provides a listing of free grants-writing websites, including guidelines from the Catalog of Federal Domestic Assistance and the Foundation Center's "Proposal Writing Short Course."

Related CRS reports are CRS Report RL34035, *Grants Work in a Congressional Office*, by Merete F. Gerli; CRS Report RL34012, *Resources for Grantseekers*, by Merete F. Gerli; and CRS Report RS21 117, *Ethical Considerations in Assisting Constituents With Grant Requests Before Federal Agencies*, by Jack Maskell.

Chapter 4 - This chapter describes key sources of information on government and private funding, and outlines eligibility for federal grants. Federal grants are intended for projects benefiting states and communities. Individuals may be eligible for other kinds of benefits or assistance, or small businesses and students may be eligible for loans. Free information is readily available to grantseekers who generally know best the details of their projects. The Catalog of Federal Domestic Assistance (CFDA) describes 1600 federal programs, 1000 of them grants, and can be searched by keyword, subject, department or agency, program title, beneficiary, and applicant eligibility. Federal department and agency web sites provide additional information and guidance, and provide state agency contacts. Once a program has been identified, eligible grantseekers may apply electronically for grants at the website Grants.gov through a uniform process for all agencies. Through Grants.gov, they may identify when federal funding notices and deadlines for a CFDA program become available, sign up for e-mail notification of funding opportunities, and track the progress of submitted applications.

Since government funds may be limited, the report also discusses sources of private and corporate foundation funding. The Foundation Center is a clearinghouse for information about private, corporate, and community foundations, with collections of resources in every state.

Included in this chapter are sources of information on writing grant proposals. See also CRS Report RL32 159, *How to Develop and Write a Grant Proposal*, by Merete F. Gerli.

Sources described in this chapter are also included in the CRS website WG02001, Grants and Federal Domestic Assistance Web Page, by Merete F. Gerli. Upon request, this website may be added to a Member's home page. For congressional staff, see also CRS Report RL34035, *Grants Work in a Congressional Office*, by Merete F. Gerli.

In: A Government Guide to Grants
Editors: Nathan E. Legaspi

ISBN: 978-1-60876-751-9
© 2010 Nova Science Publishers, Inc.

Chapter 1

BLOCK GRANTS: PERSPECTIVES AND CONTROVERSIES

Robert Jay Dilger and Eugene Boyd

SUMMARY

Block grants are a form of grant-in-aid that the federal government uses to provide state and local governments a specified amount of funding to assist them in addressing broad purposes, such as community development, social services, public health, or law enforcement. The American Recovery and Reinvestment Act of 2009 (ARRA, P.L. 111-5), which became law on February 17, 2009, provided additional funding to a number of block grant programs, including an additional $5 billion for the Temporary Assistance to Needy Families (TANF) block grant, $3.2 billion for the newest block grant program, the Energy Efficiency and Conservation Block Grant, $2 billion for Edward Byrne Memorial Justice Assistance Grants, $2 billion for the Child Care Development Block Grant, and $1 billion for the Community Development Block Grant Program.

Block grants advocates view block grants as a means to increase government efficiency and program effectiveness by redistributing power and accountability through decentralization and partial devolution of decision-making authority. Their critics view them as a means to undermine the achievement of national objectives and as a "backdoor" means to reduce government spending on domestic issues. They also claim that the decentralized nature of block grants make it difficult to measure block grant performance and to hold state and local government officials accountable for their decisions.

Block grants, which have been a part of the American federal system since 1966, are one of three general types of grants-in-aid programs: categorical grants, block grants and general revenue sharing. These grants differ along three dimensions: the range of federal control over who receives the grant, the range of recipient discretion concerning aided activities, and the type, number, detail, and scope of grant program conditions.

Categorical grants can be used only for a specifically aided program, usually are limited to narrowly defined activities, and legislation generally details the program's parameters and specifies the types of funded activities. There are four types of categorical grants: project categorical grants, formula-project categorical grants, formula categorical grants, and open-end reimbursement categorical grants.

Project categorical grants and general revenue sharing represent the ends of a continuum on the three dimensions differentiating grant types, with block grants being at the mid-point. However, there is some overlap among grant types in the middle of the continuum. For example, some block grants have characteristics normally associated with formula categorical grants. This overlap, and the variation in characteristics among block grants, helps to explain why there is some disagreement concerning precisely what is a block grant, and how many of them exist.

This chapter provides an overview of the six grant types, provides criteria for defining a block grant and uses that criteria to provide a list of current block grants, examines competing perspectives concerning the use of block grants versus other grant mechanisms to achieve national goals, provides a brief historical overview of the role of block grants in American federalism, and examines recent changes to existing block grants and proposals to create new ones.

Block grants are a form of grant-in-aid that the federal government uses to provide state and local governments a specified amount of funding to assist them in addressing broad purposes, such as community development, social services, public health, or law enforcement. The American Recovery and Reinvestment Act of 2009 (ARRA, P.L. 111-5), which became law on February 17, 2009, provided additional funding to a number of block grant programs, including an additional $5 billion for the Temporary Assistance to

Needy Families (TANF) block grant, $3.2 billion for the newest block grant program, the Energy Efficiency and Conservation Block Grant, $2 billion for Edward Byrne Memorial Justice Assistance Grants, $2 billion for the Child Care Development Block Grant, and $1 billion for the Community Development Block Grant Program.

Block grant advocates view block grants as a means to increase government efficiency and program effectiveness by redistributing power and accountability through decentralization and partial devolution of decision-making authority. Their critics view them as a means to undermine the achievement of national objectives and as a "backdoor" means to reduce government spending on domestic issues. They also claim that the decentralized nature of block grants make it difficult to measure block grant performance and to hold state and local government officials accountable for their decisions.

Block grants, which have been a part of the American federal system since 1966, are one of three general types of grants-in-aid programs: categorical grants, block grants and general revenue sharing.[1] These grants differ along three dimensions: the range of federal control over who receives the grant, the range of recipient discretion concerning aided activities, and the type, number, detail, and scope of grant program conditions.[2]

Categorical grants can be used only for a specifically aided program, usually are limited to narrowly defined activities, and legislation generally details the program's parameters and specifies the types of funded activities. There are four types of categorical grants: project categorical grants, formula-project categorical grants, formula categorical grants, and open-end reimbursement categorical grants.

Project categorical grants and general revenue sharing represent the ends of a continuum on the three dimensions differentiating grant types, with block grants being at the mid-point. However, there is some overlap among grant types in the middle of the continuum. For example, some block grants have characteristics normally associated with formula categorical grants. This overlap, and the variation in characteristics among block grants, helps to explain why there is some disagreement concerning precisely what is a block grant, and how many of them exist.

This chapter provides an overview of the six grant types, provides criteria for defining a block grant and uses that criteria to provide a list of current block grants, examines competing perspectives concerning the use of block grants versus other grant mechanisms to achieve national goals, provides a brief historical overview of the role of block grants in American federalism, and examines recent changes to existing block grants and proposals to create new ones.

GRANT DEFINITIONS

Different federal departments and agencies, including the U.S. Census Bureau, the Government Accountability Office and the U.S. Office of Management and Budget, use different definitions of grants-in-aid. However, there is agreement on the general characteristics associated with each grant type.

Of the six grant types, project categorical grants typically impose the most restraint on recipients (see **Table 1**). Federal administrators have a high degree of control over who receives projectcategorical grants (recipients must apply to the appropriate federal agency for funding and compete against other potential recipients who also meet the program's specified eligibility criteria); recipients have relatively little discretion concerning aided activities (funds must be used for narrowly specified purposes); and there is a relatively high degree of federal administrative conditions attached to the grant, typically involving the imposition of federal standards for planning, project selection, fiscal management, administrative organization, and performance.

General revenue sharing imposes the least restraint on recipients.[3] Federal administrators have a low degree of discretion over who receives general revenue sharing (funding is allocated automatically to recipients by a formula or formulas specified in legislation); recipients have broad discretion concerning aided activities; and there is a relatively low degree of federal administrative conditions attached to the grant, typically involving periodic reporting criteria and the application of standard government accounting procedures.

Block grants are at the midpoint in the continuum of recipient discretion. Federal administrators have a low degree of discretion over who receives block grants (after setting aside funding for administration and other specified activities, the remaining funds are typically allocated automatically to recipients by a formula or formulas specified in legislation); recipients have some discretion concerning aided activities (typically, funds can be used for a specified range of activities within a single functional area); and there is a moderate degree of federal administrative conditions attached to the grant, typically involving more than periodic reporting criteria and the application of standard government accounting procedures, but with fewer conditions attached to the grant than project categorical grants.

Table 1. Classification of Grant Types by Three Defining Traits

\multicolumn{4}{c}{Federal Administrator's Funding Discretion}
Low		**Medium**	**High**
Formula Categorical Grant	Block Grant	Formula-Project Categorical Grant	Project Categorical Grant
Open-ended Reimbursement Categorical Grant			
General Revenue Sharing			

\multicolumn{4}{c}{Range of Recipient's Discretion in Use of Funds}
Low		**Medium**	**High**
Project Categorical Grant		Block Grant	General Revenue Sharing
Formula-Project Categorical Grant			
Formula Categorical Grant			
Open-ended Reimbursement Categorical Grant			

\multicolumn{4}{c}{Extent of Performance Conditions}
Low		**Medium**	**High**
General Revenue Sharing		Block Grant	Project Categorical Grant

\multicolumn{4}{c}{Federal Administrator's Funding Discretion}
			Formula Categorical Grant
			Formula-Project Categorical Grant
			Open-ended Reimbursement Categorical Grant

Source: U.S. Advisory Commission on Intergovernmental Relations, *Categorical Grants: Their Role and Design*, A-52 (Washington, D.C.: U.S. GPO, 1978), p. 7.

In practice, some block grants, like TANF, have from their inception covered only a single major activity, offering programmatic flexibility within a narrow range of activities. Others started out with few program restraints, but, over time, have become "re-categorized" as Congress has chosen to limit state and local government programmatic flexibility by imposing additional administrative and reporting requirements, typically to augment congressional oversight. For example, in its examination of 11 block grants in 1995, the Government Accountability Office (GAO) found that in 9 of the 11 block grants Congress added new cost ceilings and set-asides or changed existing ones 58 times:

> These constraints often took the form of set-asides, requiring a minimum portion of funds to be used for a specific purpose, and cost-ceilings, specifying a maximum portion of funds that could be used for other purposes. This trend reduced state flexibility. Many of these restrictions were imposed because of congressional concern that states were not adequately meeting national needs.[4]

Congress has also increased programmatic flexibilities for some categorical grants, making them look increasingly like block grants. This blurring of characteristics can present challenges when analyzing the federal grants-in-aid system, as agencies and researchers may disagree over definitions and, as a result, reach different conclusions about block grants and their impact on American federalism and program performance. This blurring of characteristics should be kept in mind whenever generalizations are presented concerning the impact various grant types have on American federalism and program performance.

THE NUMBER OF BLOCK GRANTS

Congress plays a central role in shaping the scope and nature of the federal grants-in-aid system. In its deliberative, legislative role, Congress determines its objectives, decides which grant mechanism is best suited to achieve those objectives, and creates legislation to achieve its objectives, incorporating its chosen grant mechanism. It then exercises oversight to hold the administration accountable for grant implementation and to determine whether the grant is achieving its objectives.[5]

Table 2. Federal Block Grants in FY2008 (by Administering Federal Agency)

Federal Agency	Block Grant Program
Department of Agriculture[a]	Rural Community Advancement Program
Department of Education	Innovative Education Block Grant[b]
Department of Energy	Energy Efficiency and Conservation Block Grant
Department of Health and Human Services	Child Care and Development Block Grant Community Mental Health Services Block Grant Community Services Block Grant Low Income Home Energy Assistance Block Grant Maternal and Child Health Services Block Grant Preventive Health and Health Services Block Grant Social Services Block Grant Substance Abuse Prevention and Treatment Block Grant Temporary Assistance to Needy Families Title V Abstinence Education Block Grant
Department of Homeland Security	Regional Catastrophic Preparedness Grant[c] State Homeland Security Grant Urban Area Security Initiative Grant*
Department of Housing and Urban Development	Community Development Block Grant* Emergency Shelter Care[d] HOME Program* Indian Community Development Block Grant
Department of Justice	Edward Byrne Memorial Justice Assistance Grant Juvenile Accountability Block Grant* Juvenile Delinquency Prevention Block Grant
Department of Labor	Workforce Investment Act
Department of Transportation	Surface Transportation Program

Source: CRS analysis of FY2008 appropriations.

a. The table does not include Nutritional Assistance Block Grants for Puerto Rico (food stamps) because of its status as a commonwealth, and does not include Specialty Crop Block Grants authorized under Specialty Crops Competitiveness Act of 2004 (7 U.S.C. 1621) because the program does not meet the criteria used to distinguish a block grant.
b. Authorized, but no funds appropriated for FY2008. The Energy Efficiency and Conservation Block Grant has received an appropriation of $3.2 billion for FY2009.
c. Multi-state grants.
d. Funds awarded only to local governments.
e. Federally recognized tribal governments only.

The following criteria were used to determine the number of block grants that have been authorized (25) or funded (23) in FY2008 (see **Table 2**):

- eligibility is limited to state and local governments (not foreign governments or nongovernmental organizations);
- program funds are typically distributed using a formula that may be prescribed in legislation or regulations; and,
- unlike categorical programs, which target funds for a specific activity, recipients undertake, at their discretion, a number of activities within a broad functional category aimed at addressing national objectives.

Most of the block grants identified in the table award funding to state governments. Block grants that provide funding to local governments, including sub-state regional entities, either directly or through "pass-through" provisions, are identified with an asterisk (*).

The table includes two recently authorized block grants that were not funded in FY2008, the Innovative Education Block Grant program and the Energy Efficiency and Conservation Block Grant (EECBG) program. The EECBG program received an appropriation of $3.2 billion in FY2009. Given disagreements over definitions, the list of block grants presented on **Table 2** should be considered illustrative, as opposed to definitive, of the present number of block grants.

BLOCK GRANTS: COMPETING PERSPECTIVES

A federalism scholar recently suggested that efforts to enact block grants typically have been based on the following arguments:

> the national government was too large, and its elected officials and appointed officials were out of touch with grassroots needs and priorities; the federal bureaucracy was too powerful and prone to regulation; the United States Congress was too willing to preempt states and localities and to enact mandates without sufficient compensatory funding; the national government was too involved in domestic activities that were properly state or local affairs; there were too many narrow, overlapping federal grant-in-aid programs; and state governments were too often considered mere administrative subunits of the national government rather than the vital "laboratories of democracy" envisioned by Justice Louis Brandeis.[6]

He also suggested that efforts to enact block grants often met resistance in Congress because of congressional concerns about recipient's management capacity and commitment to the program, recipient's ability to make the "right" allocation choices, and the possibility that converting categorical grants to block grants might diminish both congressional and executive branch ability to provide effective program oversight. He also argued that Congress had a tendency to prefer categorical grants over block grants because they provide greater opportunity for receiving political credit.[7]

Another federalism scholar also suggested that block grant advocates have often found it difficult to gain congressional approval for block grants because their arguments have been superseded by political considerations:

> Why is it so difficult to do block granting? Why is it politically hard? And I think the answer's pretty straightforward: it seldom has more friends than it has enemies. Liberals prefer a categorical approach to intergovernmental grant giving. Essentially for two reasons: First of all, it locks in - it institutionalizes constituencies; that is, it sets up a pretty sturdy relationship between client groups; program authorizing committees in Congress; and patron agencies in the Executive Branch. And this pretty much ensures that intended target populations get funded, consistently.
>
> But, secondly, unlike block grants, which are often administered by formula, the categorical system gives politicians more opportunities for credit claiming. I'm going to quote, here from Yale political scientist David Mayhew on this subject. He says, "The categorical grant is for modern Democratic Congressmen what the Rivers and Harbors Act and the tariff were for pre-New Deal Republican Congressmen."
>
> That's true, but when the chips were down, conservatives are often not that keen about block granting, either.... They may like the fact that it may be somewhat easier to trim program spending, once programs are taken out of their political silos or cease to be entitlements. But they don't necessarily like the total lack of accountability, the absence of any strings to the money, once it goes out to the states.[8]

The following discussion examines in more detail the arguments presented by block grant advocates and block grant critics.

Block grant advocates argue that federal administrators are often out of touch with grassroots needs and priorities whereas state and local government officials are "closer to the people" than federal administrators and, therefore, are better positioned to identify state and local government needs. They also argue that state and local government officials are more "visible" to the public than federal administrators and, as a result, are more likely to be held accountable for their actions. From their perspective, this heightened level of visibility and accountability encourages state and local government officials to seek the most efficient and cost-effective means to deliver program services. As a result, they view the added flexibility provided by block grants as a means to produce both better programmatic outcomes and at a lower cost. Block grant advocates also argue that the flexibility afforded to states and localities under block grant programs allows them to innovate and experiment with new approaches to governmental challenges that would not be possible if the funding were provided through more restrictive categorical grants.[9] They argue that states have a history of learning from one another through the sharing of best practices at forums sponsored by the National Governors Association, through state and local government officials' participation in their respective national organizations' annual meetings, and through word-of-mouth.

Block grant advocates also assert that block grants promote long-term planning. Unlike project categorical grants that require state and local government officials to compete for funding, block grants use formulas to distribute funds. They argue that the use of formulas provides recipients greater assurance that funding will be continued which makes it easier for them to predict the amount of their grant and to create long-range plans for the funds' use.

Block grant advocates also claim that block grants help to address what they believe is unnecessary and wasteful duplication among existing categorical grant programs. They believe that block grants eliminate this duplication and waste by consolidating categorical grant activities, and by providing states and localities the ability to set their own priorities and allocate funds accordingly. Block grant advocates also argue that block grants will generate cost savings by reducing federal administrative costs related to state and local government paperwork requirements. However, there has been no definitive, empirical evidence that total administrative costs have been significantly reduced by converting categorical grants into block grants. Some federalism scholars have argued that costs related to "administrative overhead burdens may only have been shifted from the national to the state to the local levels through block grants."[10]

Converting entitlement programs into block grants is viewed by some as a means to eliminate what they view as uncontrollable spending. By design, entitlement program funding responds automatically to economic and demographic changes. In the short-run, enrollment in entitlement programs tends to increase during and shortly after economic recessions. In the long-run, enrollment in entitlement programs tends to increase with overall increases in eligible populations.[11] Because block grants have pre-determined funding amounts, converting entitlement programs, like Medicaid, into block grants have been seen by some as a means to impose greater fiscal discipline in the federal budget process.[12] As a federalism scholar put it:

> We face, as a nation, severe, long-term fiscal problems. We face a collision between rising costs for elderly entitlements and a shrinking revenue base.... Over time, some things, many things have to give. And I think block grants are attractive to some policy makers, as a way over a long period of time to squeeze funding for some of the big low-income programs, relative to what it would be under the current entitlement funding structures and it enables it to do it without looking heartless by proposing to throw x-numbers of people over the side in program A, B, or C.[13]

Critics of block grants argue that providing state and local government officials increased flexibility concerning the use of the program's funds reduces the ability of federal administrators and Congress to provide effective program oversight. Because block grants purposively minimize administrative requirements, there are often no federal requirements for uniform data collection, making it difficult to compare data across states and, in the view of some, rendering whatever data are available unusable for effective federal agency and congressional oversight of program performance.[14] To address this deficiency, Congress has added reporting requirements to some block grants and performance incentives that reward states for documented improvements to others.[15]

Block grant critics also assert that state and local government officials will use their increased programmatic flexibility to retarget resources away from individuals or communities with the greatest need toward those with greater political influence. They cite studies of the Community Development Block Grant program (CDBG) that found that political considerations did influence at least some local government officials when they allocated CDBG funds.[16]

Block grant advocates counter this argument by insisting that even if this was the case block grant formulas can be designed to adequately target funds to jurisdictions with the greatest need by including objective indicators of need in the distribution formula. They also point to various studies that have examined the retargeting issue and have not found evidence of significant redirection of funds. For example, a GAO study of the five block grants enacted prior to 1981 found that of the three block grant programs that had a stated objective of serving the economically needy, "there were no consistent differences between the earlier categorical programs and the pre-1981 block grants in targeting benefits to lower income people or to minority groups."[17] A study of the block grants enacted during the Reagan Administration also found that states did not use their flexibility to redirect resources away from poor or low-income families.[18] Block grant critics, however, counter these arguments by pointing out that block grant formulas often include population as a criteria of need to attract political support. From their perspective, including population in block grant formulas prevents block grants from adequately targeting assistance to needy individuals and jurisdictions.

Some block grant critics oppose the consolidation of existing categorical grants into block grants because they believe that funding for the programs is likely to diminish over time, as it is thought to be more difficult to generate political support for broad purpose, state administered programs than for categorical programs targeted at specific purposes. For example, they cite a 1995 analysis of five block grants enacted during the 1980s that found that their real (inflation-adjusted) funding level decreased from 1986 to 1995, despite a 66 percent increase in total federal grant funding during that period; and a 2003 analysis of federal funding for 11 block grants that found that their inflation-adjusted funding levels fell by an average of 11%.[19] Also, in 2006 GAO found that real per capita funding for the Community Development Block Grant (CDBG) program had declined since 1978 "by almost three-quarters from about $48 to about $13 per capita."[20] From their perspective, block grants critics view block grants as a "backdoor" means to reduce government spending on domestic issues.

Critics of block grants also contend that recipients may substitute federal block grant funds for their own financial contribution to an activity. Congress has addressed this concern by including state maintenance-of-effort provisions in grant programs which require recipients to maintain the level of funding for an activity that existed either before receiving the grant funds or over a specified period. An examination of grants-in-aid listed in the *Catalog of Federal Domestic Assistance* revealed that 33 federal grants to state and local governments have state spending maintenance-of-effort (MOE) requirements to prevent states from substituting federal funds for existing state funds. For example, the Temporary Assistance for Needy Families (TANF) block grant program requires states to maintain spending from their own funds on specified TANF or TANF-related activities at 75% of what was spent from state funds in FY1994 in TANF's predecessor programs of cash, emergency assistance, job training, and welfare-related child care spending. States are required to maintain their own spending at least at that level, and the MOE requirement increases to 80% of FY1994 spending for states that fail to meet

TANF work participation requirements. States failing to meet the MOE requirement are subject to a reduction in the state's subsequent year's block grant funding by $1 for each $1 shortfall from the required spending level.[21]

WHEN SHOULD BLOCK GRANTS BE CONSIDERED?

Since the first block grant's enactment in 1966, analysts and policymakers have tried to identify the circumstances where block grants are most desirable, and circumstances where it is appropriate to consider converting existing categorical grants into block grants. A leading federalism scholar suggested that block grants should be considered if the following conditions are present:

- when the federal government desires to supplement service levels in certain broad program areas traditionally provided under state and local jurisdiction;
- when broad national objectives are consistent with state and local program objectives;
- when the federal government seeks to establish nationwide minimum levels of service in those areas; and
- when the federal government is satisfied that state and local governments know best how to set subordinate priorities and administer the program.[22]

In the past, Congress has consolidated categorical grant programs to create new block grants. The now–defunct U.S. Advisory Commission on Intergovernmental Relations (ACIR) said that it may be appropriate to terminate or consolidate categorical programs when:

- categorical programs that are too small to have much impact or to be worth the cost of administration;
- programs do not embody essential and clear national objectives;
- programs get (or could get) most of their funding from state and local governments, or from fees for services, or that could be shifted to the private sector;[23] and
- in functional areas including health, education, and social services, that have a large number of programs; or in functional areas including justice, natural resources, and occupational health and safety, that

have a high fragmentation index score (ACIR devised a fragmentation index that measured the percentage of grant programs in a functional category (i.e., housing, transportation, etc.) relative to the percentage of federal funding allocated to programs in the functional category.).[24]

CONTEMPORARY CONTROVERSIES: PART SCORES

Block grants have been praised by some for providing state and local government officials flexibility to meet state and local needs, but are criticized by others because, in their view, accountability for results can be difficult when funding is allocated based on formulas and population counts rather than performance or meeting demonstrated need. In addition, block grants pose performance measurement challenges precisely because they can be used for a wide range of activities. The obstacles to measuring and achieving results through block grants are reflected in their Program Assessment Rating Tool (PART) scores.

PART is a set of questionnaires that the George W. Bush Administration developed to assess the effectiveness of seven different types of federal programs, in order to influence funding and management decisions. These seven "program types" include direct federal programs; competitive grant programs; block/formula grant programs; regulatory based programs; capital assets and service acquisition programs; credit programs; and research and development programs. The Obama Administration has announced that it will continue to use PART to evaluate programs, but it has indicated that it will seek changes to the questionnaires to reflect different performance goals and to ensure that "programs will not be measured in isolation, but assessed in the context of other programs that are serving the same population or meeting the same goals."[25]

PART currently focuses on four program aspects: purpose and design (20%); strategic planning (10%); program management (20%); and program results/accountability (50%).[26] Each program aspect is provided a percentage "effectiveness" rating (e.g., 85%) based on answers to a series of questions. The scores for the four program aspects are then averaged to create a single PART score. Programs are then rated, effective (193 in 2008), moderately effective (326 in 2008), adequate (297 in 2008), ineffective (26 in 2008), and results not demonstrated (173 in 2008).[27] Block grants received the lowest average score of the seven PART program types in 2008, 5% of block grant programs assessed were rated "ineffective," and 30% were rated "results not demonstrated."[28]

Block grant critics point to PART's low ratings of block grants as proof that block grants should be avoided. Block grant advocates argue that PART's heavy weighting of program results/assessment in its calculations makes PART a poor measure for assessing block grant performance. As one study concluded:

> the federal requirements ... tend to ignore the reality that many programs contain multiple goals and outcomes, rather than focusing on a single goal or outcome. These multiple goals and outcomes are often contradictory to each other. Yet PART pushes agencies to focus on single goals.... The federal efforts dealing with performance move against the devolution tide.... Efforts to hold federal government agencies accountable for the way programs are implemented actually assume that these agencies have legitimate authority to enforce the requirements that are included in performance measures.[29]

Block grant advocates also note that during his presidency President George W. Bush proposed several new block grants, despite PART's low scoring of block grant performance.

CONTEMPORARY CONTROVERSIES: FUNDING

Historically, the success or failure of block grant proposals has often been determined, in large part, on stakeholders' views of the program's future funding prospects.[30] However, in recent years, this issue has taken on even greater prominence than in the past. Prior to 1995, the primary rationale provided by block grant advocates for converting categorical grants into block grants was to eliminate program overlap and duplication and introduce greater program efficiencies by providing state and local government officials additional flexibility in program management. Since then, block grant advocates have continued to argue that converting categorical grants into block grants reduces program overlap and duplication, but they have also increasingly touted block grants as a means to control federal spending by capping expenditures and closing open-ended entitlement programs.

For example, in his FY2006 budget proposal President George W. Bush included a Strengthening America's Communities Initiative which would have combined 18 existing community and economic development programs (including the Community Development Block Grant program) into a two-part block grant. Administrative responsibility for the 18 programs would have been transferred from five federal agencies (the Department of Housing and Urban Development, the Economic Development Administration in the Department of Commerce, the Department of the Treasury, the Department of Health and Human Services, and the Department of Agriculture) to the Department of Commerce, which administers the programs of the Economic Development Administration. Under the proposal, the Department of Commerce would have administered a core block grant program and a bonus program. The bonus program would have awarded additional funds to communities that demonstrated efforts to improve economic conditions. The proposal would have reduced total funding for the 18 programs from $5.6 billion in FY2005 to $3.7 billion in FY2006. Congress rejected the Administration's budget proposal and funded all 18 programs at a total level of $5.3 billion.[31]

The recent increased emphasis on capping expenditures and closing previously open-ended entitlement programs has changed the nature of congressional considerations of what some have labeled "new-style" block grant proposals. During their deliberations, instead of focusing primarily on questions concerning state and local government administrative and fiscal capacity and commitment to the program, Congress has increasingly focused on the short- and long-term budgetary implications of block grants, both for the federal budget and for recipients. Some have argued that the new-style block grants send a mixed message to state and local government officials, providing them added programmatic authority, flexibility in administration, and greater freedom to innovate, but at the cost of restrained federal financial support and increased performance expectations.[32]

APPENDIX. BRIEF HISTORY OF BLOCK GRANTS

H.R. 5686, The Public Welfare Act of 1946, introduced by Representative Aime J. Forand, D-RI, as an amendment to the Social Security Act, is the first known congressional effort to enact a block grant. It would have allowed states to continue providing public welfare assistance in "the present categories of old-age assistance, aid to dependent children, and aid to the blind, or whether they preferred to provide for these groups as part of a comprehensive assistance program" with choices about program design left to the states.[33]

In 1949, the Commission on the Organization of the Executive Branch of the Government, known as the Hoover Commission in honor of its chair, Herbert Hoover, further raised awareness of the block grant concept by recommending that "a system of grants be established based upon broad categories – such as highways, education, public assistance and public health – as contrasted with the present system of extensive fragmentation."[34] However, Congress did not create the first block grant until 1966 for comprehensive health care services (now the Preventive Health and Health Services Block Grant) in The Partnership for Public Health Act of 1966. It replaced nine formula categorical grants.[35] Two years later, Congress created the second block grant, the Law Enforcement Assistance Administration's Grants for Law Enforcement program (sometimes referred to as the "Crime Control" or "Safe Streets" block grant) in the Omnibus Crime Control and Safe Streets Act of 1968.[36] Unlike the health care services block grant, it was created *de novo*, and did not consolidate any existing categorical grants.[37]

In his 1971 State of the Union speech, President Richard M. Nixon announced a plan to consolidate 129 federal grant programs in six functional areas, 33 in education, 26 in transportation, 12 in urban community development, 17 in manpower training, 39 in rural community development, and 2 in law enforcement into what he called six "special revenue sharing" programs. Unlike the categorical grants they would replace, the proposed special revenue sharing programs had no state matching requirements, relatively few auditing or oversight requirements, and the funds were distributed automatically by formula without prior federal approval of plans for their use.[38]

The education, transportation, rural community development, and law enforcement proposals failed to gain congressional approval, primarily because they generated opposition from interest groups affiliated with the programs who worried that the programs' future funding would be compromised.[39] Nonetheless, the Nixon Administration's efforts led to the adoption of three more block grants, the first was signed by President Nixon and the remaining two were signed by President Gerald R. Ford.

The Comprehensive Employment and Training Assistance Block Grant program was created by the Comprehensive Employment and Training Act of 1973. It merged 17 existing manpower training categorical grant programs. The Community Development Block Grant program (and its affiliated Indian Community Development Block Grant program which is funded through a set-aside of the Community Development Block Grant's formula funds) was created by the Housing and Community Development Act of 1974. It consolidated six existing community and economic development categorical grant programs.[40] Title XX social services, later renamed the Social Services Block Grant program, was created *de novo* and, therefore, did not consolidate any existing categorical grant programs. It was authorized by the 1974 amendments of the Social Security Act which was signed into law on January 4, 1975.[41]

Congress did not approve any additional block grants until 1981. President Ronald Reagan had proposed consolidating 85 existing elementary and secondary education, public health, social services, emergency assistance (for low-income energy assistance and emergency welfare assistance), and community development categorical grants into seven block grants (two in elementary and secondary education, two in public health, and one each for social services, emergency assistance, and community development). He also recommended that the programs' funding be reduced 25%, arguing that the administrative savings brought about by the conversion to block grants would largely offset the budget reduction. Congress subsequently adopted the Omnibus Budget and Reconciliation Act of 1981 which consolidated 75 categorical grant programs and two existing block grants into the following nine new, or revised, block grants:

- Elementary and Secondary Education (37 categorical grants),
- Alcohol, Drug Abuse, and Mental Health Services (10 categorical grants),
- Maternal and Child Health Services (9 categorical grants),
- Preventive Health and Human Services Block Grant (merged 6 categorical grants with the Health Incentive Grants for Comprehensive Health Services Block Grant),
- Primary Care (2 categorical grants),
- Community Services (7 categorical grants),
- Social Services (one categorical grant and the Social Services for Low Income and Public Assistance Recipients Block Grant),
- Low-Income Home Energy Assistance (1 categorical grant), and
- revised the Community Development Block Grant program (adding an existing discretionary grant and 3 categorical grants).[42]

Overall, funding for the categorical grants bundled into these block grants was reduced 12%, about $1 billion, from their combined funding level the previous year.[43]

In retrospect, some federalism scholars consider these block grants as more "historical accidents than carefully conceived restructurings of categorical programs" because they were contained in a lengthy bill that was adopted under special parliamentary rules requiring a straight up or down vote without the possibility of amendment, the bill was designed to reduce the budget deficit not to reform federalism relationships, and the bill was not considered and approved by authorizing committees of jurisdiction.[44] Nonetheless, largely due to the Omnibus Budget and Reconciliation Act of 1981, in FY1 984 there were 12 block grants in operation (compared to 392 categorical grants), accounting for about 15% of total grants-in-aid funding.[45]

During the first six years of his presidency, President Ronald Reagan submitted 32 block grant proposals to Congress, with nine created by the Omnibus Budget and Reconciliation Act of 1981 and the Federal Transit Capital and Operating Assistance Block Grant added in 1982. In addition, the Job Training Partnership Act of 1982 created a new block grant for job training that replaced the block grant contained in the Comprehensive Employment and Training Act of 1973.[46]

Federalism scholars generally agree that President Reagan had unprecedented success in achieving congressional approval for block grants. However, they also note that most of President Reagan's block grant proposals failed to gain congressional approval, primarily because they were opposed by organizations who feared that, if enacted, the block grants would result in less funding for the affected programs. For example, in 1982, President Reagan proposed, but could not get congressional approval for, a $20 billion "swap" in which the federal government would return to states full responsibility for funding Aid to Families With Dependent Children (AFDC) (now Temporary Assistance for Needy Families) and food stamps in exchange for federal assumption of state contributions for Medicaid. As part of the deal, he also proposed a temporary $28 billion trust fund or "super revenue sharing program" to replace 43 other federal grant programs. Both the swap proposal and the proposed devolution of 43 federal grants were opposed by organizations who feared that, if enacted, they would result in less funding for the affected programs. For example, the National Governors Association supported the federal take over of Medicaid, but objected to assuming the costs for AFDC and food stamps. The economy was weakening at that time and governors worried that they would not have the fiscal capacity necessary to support the programs without continued federal assistance.[47]

From 1983 until 1995, Congress approved six new block grants: the Community Youth Activity Block Grant (1988), Child Care and Development

Block Grant (1990), the HOME Investment Partnerships Program (1990), the Surface Transportation Program (1991), Substance Abuse Prevention and Treatment Block Grant (1992), and the Community Mental Health Services Block Grant (1992).[48] Established by the Intermodal Surface Transportation Efficiency Act of 1991, the Surface Transportation Program had, by far, the largest budget of any block grant program at that time, with $17.5 billion appropriated in FY1993. Three block grants were terminated during this period: Community Youth Activity Program, Law Enforcement Assistance, and Alcohol, Drug Abuse, and Mental Health (which was broken into two new block grants, the Community Mental Health Services Block Grant and the Prevention and Treatment of Substance Abuse Block Grant, in 1992). According to the now defunct U.S. Advisory Commission on Intergovernmental Relations, there were 15 block grants in operation in 1995 (23 block grants had been enacted, four were converted into other block grants, and four were eliminated), and 618 categorical grants.[49] In FY1995, block grants accounted for about 14% of the $228 billion in federal grants-in-aid assistance.[50]

In 1996, the open-ended entitlement categorical grant, Aid to Families with Dependent Children was converted into the Temporary Assistance to Needy Families (TANF) block grant by the Personal Responsibility and Work Opportunity Reconciliation Act of 1996. Funded at $16.7 billion annually, TANF rivaled the Surface Transportation Program for the largest budget of all the block grants. Like some other block grants, TANF "was a hybrid program balancing stringent federal standards against significant state flexibility."[51] Funding ($424 million) was also provided for a Local Law Enforcement Block Grant which had been authorized the previous year in the Local Law Enforcement Block Grant Act of 1995.[52]

In 1998, the Juvenile Accountability Block Grant program was created by the FY1998 Department of Justice Appropriations Act, and later codified by the 21st Century Department of Justice Reauthorization Act of 2002. It provides funding for 16 accountability-based purpose areas, including, but not limited to, implementing graduated sanctions; building or operating juvenile correction or detention facilities; hiring juvenile court officers, including judges, probation officers, and special advocates; and hiring additional juvenile prosecutors. The 21st Century Department of Justice Reauthorization Act of 2002 also consolidated several pre-existing categorical grant programs into the Juvenile Delinquency Prevention Block Grant program. It provides funding for a wide array of services, treatments, and interventions, including, but not limited to projects that provide treatment to juvenile offenders and at risk juveniles who are victims of child abuse or neglect, or who have experienced violence at home, at school, or in their communities; and educational projects or support services for juveniles that focus on encouraging juveniles to stay in school; aiding in the transition from school to work; and encouraging new approaches to preventing school violence and vandalism.[53]

Prior to the September 11, 2001 terrorist attacks and the subsequent creation of the Department of Homeland Security, the federal government had three categorical grants-in-aid programs pertinent to homeland security: the State Domestic Preparedness program administered by the Department of Justice, the Emergency Management Performance Grant program administered by the Federal Emergency Management Agency, and the Metropolitan Medical Response System administered by the Department of Health and Human Services. There are now 17 federal grant programs administered by the Grant Programs Directorate within the Federal Emergency Management Agency in the Department of Homeland Security, including 14 categorical grant programs and the following three block grant programs: State Homeland Security Grants, formerly called the State Domestic Preparedness Program, (created in 2003), Urban Area Security Initiative Grants (created in 2003), and the Regional Catastrophic Preparedness Grant (created in 2008).[54]

In 2005, the Violence Against Women and Department of Justice Reauthorization Act of 2005 combined the Edward Byrne Memorial State and Local Law Enforcement Assistance programs and the Local Law Enforcement Block Grant program into the Edward Byrne Memorial Justice Assistance Grant program. Its funds can be used for seven broad purposes: law enforcement, prosecution and court programs, prevention and education programs, corrections and community corrections programs, drug treatment programs, planning, evaluation, and technology improvement programs, and crime victim and witness programs (other than compensation).[55]

The American Recovery and Reinvestment Act of 2009 included $3.2 billion for the newest block grant, the Energy Efficiency and Conservation Block Grant (EECBG) program, for FY2009. The EECBG program was authorized by the Energy Independence and Security Act of 2007, but it was not appropriated any funding. It provides federal grants to local governments, Indian tribes, states, and U.S. territories to reduce energy use and fossil fuel emissions, and for improvements in energy efficiency.[56]

End Notes

[1] The first block grant, for comprehensive health care services, was created in The Partnership for Public Health Act of 1966. It replaced nine formula categorical grants (see **Appendix**).

[2] U.S. Advisory Commission on Intergovernmental Relations (ACIR), *Categorical Grants: Their Role and Design*, A52 (Washington, D.C.: U.S. GPO, 1978), p. 5.

[3] General revenue sharing distributed funds to states from 1972-1981 and to localities from 1972-1986. The federal government currently does not have a general revenue sharing program.

[4] U.S. General Accounting Office, *Block Grants: Characteristics, Experience, and Lessons Learned* (Washington, D.C.: U.S. GPO, February 1995), pp. 8-11.

[5] ACIR, *Categorical Grants: Their Role and Design*, A-52 (Washington, D.C.: U.S. GPO, 1978), p. 61.

[6] Carl W. Stenberg, "Block Grants and Devolution," in *Intergovernmental Management for the 21st Century*, eds. Paul Posner and Timothy Conlan (Washington, D.C.: The Brookings Institution Press, 2007), p. 263.

[7] Ibid., pp. 267, 271-274.

[8] Pietro Nivola, Comments at a forum on "Block Grants: Past, Present, and Prospects," The Brookings Institution, Washington, D.C., October 15, 2003, http://www.brookings.edu/comm/events/20031015_panel2.pdf.

[9] ACIR, *Block Grants: A Comparative Analysis*, A-60 (Washington, D.C.: U.S. GPO, 1977), pp. 8-11.

[10] Carl W. Stenberg, "Block Grants and Devolution," in *Intergovernmental Management for the 21st Century*, eds. Paul Posner and Timothy Conlan (Washington, D.C.: The Brookings Institution Press, 2007), p. 273.

[11] Kenneth Finegold, Laura Wherry, and Stephanie Schardin, "Block Grants: Details of the Bush Proposals," *New Federalism: Issues and Options for States* (Washington, D.C.: The Urban Institute, April 2004), p. 6.

[12] Jeanne M. Lambrew, "Making Medicaid a Block Grant Program: An Analysis of the Implications of Past Proposals," *The Milbank Quarterly* 83:1 (2005), p. 43.

[13] Robert Greenstein, Comments at a forum on "Block Grants: Past, Present, and Prospects," The Brookings Institution, Washington, D.C., October 15, 2003, http://www.brookings.edu/comm/events/20031015_panel2.pdf.

[14] Kenneth Finegold, Laura Wherry, and Stephanie Schardin, "Block Grants: Details of the Bush Proposals," *New Federalism: Issues and Options for States* (Washington, D.C.: The Urban Institute, April 2004), p. 9.

[15] U.S. General Accounting Office, *Block Grants: Characteristics, Experience, and Lessons Learned* (Washington, D.C.: U.S. GPO, February 1995), pp. 7, 9-11.

[16] Donald Kettl, "Can the Cities be Trusted? The Community Development Experience," *Political Science Quarterly* 94:3 (Autumn 1979), pp. 437-451; and Howard Stern, "Can the Mayors Be Trusted? Using Community Development Block Grants to Get Re-elected," Paper presented at the 62nd Annual Meeting of the Midwest Political Science Association, April 15-18, 2004, Chicago, Il,
http://www.allacademic.com//meta/p_mla_apa_research_citation/0/8/3/6/1/pages83613/p83613-2.php.

[17] U.S. General Accounting Office, *Lessons Learned from Past Block Grants: Implications for Congressional Oversight*, GAO/IPE-82-8 (Washington, D.C.: U.S. GPO, September 23, 1982), p. ii.

[18] George E. Peterson, Randall R. Bovbjerg, Barbara A. Davis, Walter G. Davis, Eugene C. Durham, and Theresa A. Guillo, *The Reagan Block Grants: What Have We Learned?* (Washington, D.C.: Urban Institute Press, 1986), pp. 18-21.

[19] Kenneth Finegold, Laura Wherry, and Stephanie Schardin, "Block Grants: Historical Overview and Lessons Learned," *New Federalism: Issues and Options for States* (Washington, D.C.: The Urban Institute, April 2004), p. 4.

[20] U.S. Government Accountability Office (GAO), *Community Development Block Grant Formula: Options for Improving the Targeting of Funds*, GAO-06-904T 8 (Washington, D.C.: U.S. GPO, June 27, 2006), p. 2.

[21] For further analysis, see CRS Report RL32748, *The Temporary Assistance for Needy Families (TANF) Block Grant: A Primer on TANF Financing and Federal Requirements*, by Gene Falk.

[22] U.S. Congress, Joint Economic Committee, Subcommittee on Joint Economic Goals and Intergovernmental Policy, Prepared statement of David B. Walker, Assistant Director, U.S. Advisory Commission on Intergovernmental Relations, *Block Grants and the Intergovernmental System*, 97th Cong., 1st sess., July 15, 1981 (Washington: GPO, 1981), pp. 47-48.

[23] ACIR, *An Agenda for American Federalism: Restoring Confidence and Competence* (Washington, D.C.: U.S. GPO, 1981), pp. 111-112.

[24] ACIR, *Federal Grant Programs in Fiscal Year 1982: Their Numbers, Sizes, and Fragmentation Indexes in Historical Perspective* (Washington, D.C.: U.S. GPO, 1983), p. 2.

[25] U.S. Office of Management and Budget, *A New Era of Responsibility: Renewing America's Promise* (Washington, D.C.: U.S. GPO, 2009), p. 39, *http://www.whitehouse.gov/omb/assets*

[26] For further analysis, see CRS Report RL32663, *The Bush Administration's Program Assessment Rating Tool (PART)*, by Clinton T. Brass.

[27] U.S. Office of Management and Budget, ExpectMore.Gov website, http://www.whitehouse.gov/omb/expectmore/about.html.

[28] U.S. Office of Management and Budget, *Budget of the United States, FY2009 Analytical Perspectives: Crosscutting Programs* (Washington, D.C.: U.S. GPO, 2009), p. 112, http://www.whitehouse.gov/omb/budget/fy2009/pdf/apers/crosscutting.pdf.

[29] Beryl Radin, "Performance Management and Intergovernmental Relations," in *Intergovernmental Management for the 21st Century*, eds. Paul Posner and Timothy Conlan (Washington, D.C.: The Brookings Institution Press, 2007), pp. 244, 251.

[30] Timothy Conlan, *New Federalism: Intergovernmental Reform From Nixon to Reagan* (Washington, D.C.: The Brookings Institution, 1988), pp. 172-178.

[31] For further analysis, see CRS Report RL32823, *An Overview of the Administration's Strengthening America's Communities Initiative*, by Eugene Boyd et al.

[32] Carl W. Stenberg, "Block Grants and Devolution: A Future Tool?" in *Intergovernmental Management for the 21st Century*, eds. Timothy J. Conlan and Paul L. Posner (Washington, D.C.: Brookings Institution Press, 2008), p. 271.

[33] U.S. Congress, House Committee on Ways and Means, *Amendments to Social Security Act*, Hearing on Social Security Legislation, 79th Cong., 2nd sess., May 6, 1946 (Washington: GPO, 1946), p. 1046; and George E. Peterson, Randall R. Bovbjerg, Barbara A. Davis, Walter G. Davis, Eugene C. Durham, and Theresa A. Guillo, *The Reagan Block Grants: What Have We Learned?* (Washington, D.C.: Urban Institute Press, 1986), p. 2.

[34] U.S. Congress, House Committee on Expenditures in the Executive Departments, *Overseas Administration, Federal-State Relations, Federal Research: Letter from the Chairman, Commission on the Organization of the Executive Branch of the Government*, committee print, 81st Cong., 1st sess., March 25, 1949, H. Prt. 81-140 (Washington: GPO, 1949), p. 36.

[35] David B. Walker, *The Rebirth of Federalism: Slouching Toward Washington* (Chatham, NJ: Chatham House Publishers, Inc., 1995), pp. 70-71; and Kenneth T. Palmer, "The Evolution of Grant Policies," in *The Changing Politics of Federal Grants*, eds. Lawrence D. Brown, James W. Fossett and Kenneth T. Palmer (Washington, D.C.: The Brookings Institution Press, 1984), pp. 18-20.

[36] Carl W. Stenberg, "Block Grants and Devolution: A Future Tool?" in *Intergovernmental Management for the 21st Century*, eds. Timothy J. Conlan and Paul L. Posner (Washington, D.C.: Brookings Institution Press, 2008), p. 266.

[37] ACIR, *The Future of Federalism in the 1980s*, M-126 (Washington, D.C.: U.S. GPO, July 1980), p. 51.

[38] Claude E. Barfield, *Rethinking Federalism: Block Grants and Federal, State, and Local Responsibilities* (Washington, D.C.: American Enterprise Institute for Public Policy Research, 1981), p. 3.

[39] Timothy Conlan, *From New Federalism to Devolution: Twenty-Five Years of Intergovernmental Reform* (Washington, D.C.: The Brookings Institution, 1998), p. 62.

[40] Note: Most sources indicate that CDBG merged 7 categorical grant programs. However, one of the categorical grant programs initially designated for consolidation, the Section 312 Housing Rehabilitation Loan program, was retained as a separate program. See ACIR, *Block Grants: A Comparative Analysis*, A-60 (Washington, D.C.: U.S. GPO, 1977), p. 7.

[41] Carl W. Stenberg, "Block Grants and Devolution: A Future Tool?" in *Intergovernmental Management for the 21st Century*, eds. Timothy J. Conlan and Paul L. Posner (Washington, D.C.: Brookings Institution Press, 2008), p. 266; ACIR, *In Respect to Realities: A Report on Federalism in 1975*, M-103 (Washington, D.C.: U.S. GPO, April 1976), pp 16-20; and ACIR, *Block Grants: A Comparative Analysis*, A-60 (Washington, D.C.: U.S. GPO, 1977), pp. 15-40. Note: Title XX initially had all of the characteristics of a block grant and ACIR counted it as a block grant since its inception, but it was not formally called a block grant program until 1981.

[42] David B. Walker, Albert J. Richter, and Cynthia Colella, "The First Ten Months: Grant-In-Aid, Regulatory, and Other Changes," *Intergovernmental Perspective* 8:1 (Winter 1982), pp. 5-11.

[43] U.S. General Accounting Office, *Block Grants: Characteristics, Experience and Lessons Learned*, GAO/HEHS-95- 74, February 9, 1995, p. 2, http://www.gao.gov/archive/1995/he95074.pdf. Note: the funding reductions ranged from a $159 million, or 30%, reduction in the Community Services Block Grant to a $94 million, or 10%, increase in funding for the Community Development Block Grant program.

[44] Carl W. Stenberg, "Block Grants and Devolution: A Future Tool?" in *Intergovernmental Management for the 21st Century*, eds. Timothy J. Conlan and Paul L. Posner (Washington, D.C.: Brookings Institution Press, 2008), p. 267; and Timothy Conlan, *From New Federalism to Devolution: Twenty-Five Years of Intergovernmental Reform* (Washington, D.C.: The Brookings Institution, 1998), pp. 110-121.

[45] ACIR, *A Catalog of Federal Grant-In-Aid Programs to State and Local Governments: Grants Funded FY1984*, M139 (Washington, D.C.: U.S. GPO, 1984), pp. 1-3.

[46] Ibid., p. 3; Timothy Conlan, *From New Federalism to Devolution: Twenty-Five Years of Intergovernmental Reform* (Washington, D.C.: The Brookings Institution, 1998), p. 142; and CRS Report 87-845, *Block Grants: Inventory and Funding History*, Sandra S. Osbourn, November 21, 1986, available by request.

[47] Timothy J. Conlan and David B. Walker, "Reagan's New Federalism: Design, Debate and Discord," *Intergovernmental Perspective* 8:4 (Winter 1983): 6-15, 18-22; and Timothy Conlan, *New Federalism: Intergovernmental Reform From Nixon to Reagan* (Washington, D.C.: The Brookings Institution, 1988), pp. 182-198.

[48] For further analysis, see CRS Report RL30785, *The Child Care and Development Block Grant: Background and Funding*, by Melinda Gish; CRS Report R40118, *An Overview of the HOME Investment Partnerships Program*, by Katie Jones; CRS Report R40053, *Surface Transportation Program Reauthorization Issues for the 111th Congress*, coordinated by John W. Fischer; and CRS Report RL33997, *Substance Abuse and Mental Health Services Administration (SAMHSA):Reauthorization Issues*, by Ramya Sundararaman.

[49] Carl W. Stenberg, "Block Grants and Devolution: A Future Tool?" in *Intergovernmental Management for the 21st Century*, eds. Timothy J. Conlan and Paul L. Posner (Washington,

D.C.: Brookings Institution Press, 2008), p. 267; and ACIR, *A Catalog of Federal Grant-In-Aid Programs to State and Local Governments: Grants Funded FY1995*, M-195 (Washington, D.C.: U.S. GPO, 1995), pp. iii, 1-3.

[50] U.S. General Accounting Office, *Block Grants: Characteristics, Experience, and Lessons Learned* (Washington, D.C.: U.S. GPO, February 1995), pp. 2, 26.

[51] Carl W. Stenberg, "Block Grants and Devolution: A Future Tool?" in *Intergovernmental Management for the 21st Century*, eds. Timothy J. Conlan and Paul L. Posner (Washington, D.C.: Brookings Institution Press, 2008), pp. 268, 269. For further analysis, see CRS Report RL32748, *The Temporary Assistance for Needy Families (TANF) Block Grant: A Primer on TANF Financing and Federal Requirements*, by Gene Falk and CRS Report RL32760, *The Temporary Assistance for Needy Families (TANF) Block Grant: Responses to Frequently Asked Questions*, by Gene Falk.

[52] U.S. Department of Justice, Office of Justice Programs, *Local Law Enforcement Block Grant Program, 1996-2004* (Washington, D.C.: U.S. Department of Justice, September 2004), p. 1.

[53] For further analysis, see CRS Report RL33 947, *Juvenile Justice: Legislative History and Current Legislative Issues*, by Blas Nuñez-Neto.

[54] For further analysis, see CRS Report R40246, *Department of Homeland Security Assistance to States and Localities: A Summary and Issues for the 111th Congress*, by Shawn Reese; and CRS Report RL33770, *Department of Homeland Security Grants to State and Local Governments: FY2003 to FY2006*, by Steven Maguire and Shawn Reese.

[55] For further analysis, see CRS Report RS22416, *Edward Byrne Memorial Justice Assistance Grant Program: Legislative and Funding History*, by Nathan James.

[56] U.S. Department of Energy, "Energy Efficiency and Conservation Block Grants," http://apps1.eere.energy. For further analysis, see CRS Report R40412, *Energy Provisions in the American Recovery and Reinvestment Act of 2009 (P.L. 111-5)*, coordinated by Fred Sissine.

In: A Government Guide to Grants
Editors: Nathan E. Legaspi

ISBN: 978-1-60876-751-9
© 2010 Nova Science Publishers, Inc.

Chapter 2

GRANTS WORK IN A CONGRESSIONAL OFFICE

Merete F. Gerli

SUMMARY

Members of Congress receive frequent requests from grant seekers needing funds for projects in districts and states. The congressional office should first determine its priorities regarding the appropriate assistance to give constituents, from providing information on grants programs to active advocacy of projects. Congressional grants staff can best help grant seekers by first themselves gaining some understanding of the grants process.

Each office handles grants requests in its own way, depending upon the Member's legislative agenda and overall organization and workload. There may be a full-time grants specialist or several staff members under the supervision of a grants coordinator working solely in the area of grants and projects. In some offices, all grants requests are handled in the district or state office; in others, they are answered by the Washington, DC, staff.

To assist grant seekers applying for federal funds, congressional offices can develop working relationships with grants officers in federal and state departments and agencies. Because more than 90% of federal funds go to state and local governments that, in turn, manage federal grants and sub-award to applicants in their state, congressional staff need to identify their own state administering offices. For example, much of the current economic stimulus funding (see the website Recovery.gov at http://www.recovery) is being allocated through existing grants-in- aid programs.

To educate constituents, a congressional office may sometimes provide selected grant seekers information on funding opportunities; or may sponsor seminars on federal and private assistance. Because most funding resources are on the Internet, Member home pages can also link to grants sources such as the *Catalog of Federal Domestic Assistance* and *Grants.gov* so that constituents themselves can search for grants and funding opportunities. The CRS Web page, *Grants and Federal Domestic Assistance*, Merete F. Gerli (see sample at http://www.crs.gov/reference/ general/grants/member-grant.html), can be added to a Member's home page upon request, and is updated automatically on House and Senate servers. Another CRS Web page, *Grants, Business Opportunities, and Student Financial Aid*, by Mereti F. Gerli, at http://www.crs.gov/reference/ general/WG02001.shtml, covers key CRS products.

Congressional staff can use CRS reports to learn about grants work and to provide information on government and private funding. In addition to the current report, these include CRS Report RS21 117, *Ethical Considerations in Assisting Constituents With Grant Requests Before Federal Agencies*, by Jack Maskell; CRS Report RL34012, *Resources for Grantseekers*, by Merete F. Gerli; and CRS Report RL32 159, *How to Develop and Write a Grant Proposal*, by Merete F. Gerli. CRS also offers reports on block grants and the appropriations process; federal assistance for homeland security and terrorism preparedness; and federal programs on specific subjects and for specific groups, such as state and local governments, police and fire departments, libraries and museums, nonprofit organizations, small business, and other topics. An internal grants manual outlining office policies and procedures should be developed to help grants staff. With reductions in federal programs, grants specialists should also become familiar with other funding, such as private or corporate foundations, as alternatives or supplements to federal grants.

INTRODUCTION

Members of Congress receive numerous requests from grant seekers, including state and local governments, nonprofit social service and community action organizations, private research groups, small businesses, and individuals, for information and help in obtaining funds for projects. Both government and private foundation funding may be appropriate.

For example, the American Recovery and Reconstruction Act (ARRA, P.L. 111-5) is providing $787 billion through a vast array of discretionary and mandatory spending and tax provisions. Funds are distributed to states, localities, other entities and individuals through a combination of formula and competitive grants and direct assistance.

Federal grants are not benefits or entitlements to individuals. Most federal funding goes to state and local governments, which in turn sub-award to local entities such as nonprofit organizations. Grants may be available for projects serving communities and needs. For example, government assistance may be available for nonprofit organizations, including faith-based groups, for initiatives such as establishing soup kitchens or after-school programs benefitting entire communities; and local governments seeking funds for community services, infrastructure, and economic revitalization may be most eligible for state and federal funds.

Congressional offices may often need to direct constituents seeking government aid to funding options other than grants. Community fund-raising may be most suitable for school enrichment activities such as field trips or for band or sports uniforms. Local business or foundation funding might be more appropriate for supporting projects such as construction of local memorials or commemorative programs. For others, such as for starting or expanding a small business or for students, loans may be available.

- Individuals looking for government benefits may find useful the website GovBenefits.gov at http://www.govbenefits.gov.
- Students seeking financial aid should search the Department of Education website at http://Studentaid.ed.gov.
- To start or expand a small business, the federal government provides assistance in the form of loans, advisory, or technical assistance. See the Small Business Administration website at http://www.sba.gov.
- To respond to constituents who have seen ads promising federal grants for personal expenses, refer them to the Federal Trade Commission Consumer Alert "Free Government Grants: Don't Take Them For Grant-ed" (September 2006) at *http://www.ftc.gov/ bcp/edu/pubs/consumer/alerts/alt134.shtm;* and the Better Business Bureau article "Need a Bailout? Don't Look to Grants for Your

Answer," The Business Monthly (March 2009) at *http://www.bizmonthly.com/ 3 2009/17.shtml*.

Given the competition for federal funds, the success rate in obtaining federal assistance is limited. A grants staff's effectiveness often depends on both an understanding of the grants process and on the relations it establishes with federal departments and agencies, with state grants administering agencies (SAA's), private and local foundations, and other contacts.

This chapter does not constitute a blueprint for every office involved in grants and projects activity, nor does it present in-depth information about all aspects of staff activity in this area. The discussion describes some basics about the grants process and some of the approaches and techniques used by congressional offices in dealing with this type of constituent service.

ORGANIZING OFFICE GRANTS OPERATIONS

Senate and House offices allocate staff and other resources to grants and projects activities in order to assist the constituents with projects of potential benefit to their districts, cities, or states. Each congressional office handles grants requests in its own way, depending upon such factors as the Member's philosophy on federal support for local projects, the relation of certain proposals to his or her legislative activity, or the Member's particular interest in specific locations or types of projects. Other factors may include the degree of economic distress in any given locality and the current level of federal assistance it receives.

Grants activities in any congressional office depend very much upon the overall organization, staff, and workload of the office.

- Most offices divide responsibility by function (i.e., legislation is assigned to legislative assistants and correspondents, media relations and newsletters are handles by a press secretary, and caseworkers help with problems of individuals). Offices organized in this way may have a full-time grants specialist or several staff members under the supervision of a grants coordinator working solely in the area of grants and projects.
- Some offices divide responsibilities by subject area (i.e., a specialist in health issues is involved with legislation, correspondence,

casework, grants, projects, speeches, and press releases in that subject area).
- DC, state, or district office? In some offices, all grants requests are handled in the district or state office; in others, they are answered by the Washington, DC, staff; still others divide grants and projects activity between the district or state office and the Washington, DC, office. Regardless of how this responsibility is assigned, it is helpful to have at least one person in the district or state office and one person in the Washington, DC, office familiar with the whole process. District or state staff may be more readily able to communicate and develop relationships with federal state and federal regional offices, or state administering agencies, often the preferred contact office for federal programs.
- State delegation cooperation. Since some constituents request the aid of the entire state delegation for a grant or project, cooperation among Members of the delegation can minimize duplication of effort and permit more effective use of staff time. To increase the chances of a project's funding, Members may solicit the support of other Members either from the same geographic region if the proposal would benefit a wide area, or from those who hold key positions in leadership or on committees which exercise funding and oversight of the federal program. Political considerations can limit the amount of such cooperation. One state's delegation has established a State Projects Office to help its constituents learn about the grants process and follow through on all applications until awards are made.

The grants person in the congressional office can serve constituents not only as a source of information but also as a facilitator with agencies and foundations and, in some cases, even as an advocate. The congressional office is seen by constituents as a potential source of assistance, which includes

- providing facts about financial and nonfinancial assistance available through federal programs;
- clarifying the intricacies of proposal development, application, and follow-up procedures;
- writing letters of interest or support from the Member to the granting agency once a grant proposal is ready for submission;
- resolving problems that occur when an applicant is unsuccessful in obtaining funds or other assistance; and

- suggesting other sources for grant assistance in both the private and public sectors.

The congressional office should first determine the priorities of its particular office:

- assess the volume of incoming grants requests;
- determine criteria for how much attention should be given to each grants request (e.g., number of people who will be affected, visibility of projects, or political implications);
- decide the role of the congressional office: information source or active advocacy, or sometimes even earmarking appropriations for a project that mirrors the Member's legislative agenda.

Congressional grants staff can help their constituents best when they thoroughly understand the entire grants process:

- defining the project;
- searching for likely funding sources;
- developing and writing proposals;
- applying for grants;
- understanding review and award procedures; and
- knowing post-award requirements.

Managing Grants Requests

To assure continuity, particularly in cases of staff turnover and shifting responsibilities, and to monitor the progress of the grants and projects operation, several resources can be developed. Commercial computer software packages are available to manage correspondence, projects, and workload. Congressional office systems administrators should contact House Information Resources (ext. 56002) or the Senate Sergeant at Arms' Help Desk (ext. 41517) for recommendations.

Office Grants Manual

An internal grants manual is a valuable tool for grants staff to develop. It can outline office policies and procedures and ensure continuity when staff changes. Among the items that might be included in such a manual are as follows:

- a statement of the Member's policy on letters of endorsement and press announcements, along with samples.
- a checklist of procedures to facilitate the training of new staff.
- sample project worksheets, allowing space for agency contacts, status reports, and follow-up timetables.
- a constantly updated telephone and email listing of contacts in federal, state, and local agencies, and foundations that have proven especially helpful.

File Systems and Logs

A congressional office may wish to maintain detailed, cross-referenced files such as agency files, constituent files by county, and tracking records.

Agency Files

- Agency files, which could also be arranged under broad subjects, or use subject subdivisions: for example, Defense Department, district contracts; Education Department, curriculum development; Justice Department, Community Oriented Policing (COPS) program.
- Program files, which include detailed information on the most frequently used programs in communities in the state or district, with a fact sheet describing each program, plus agency brochures, and contacts.
- Project files, which may contain lists of applicants for each project. Some offices keep records on the steps taken in support of all grant applications as documentation.

Constituent Files by County

- These can prove especially useful for the Member's visits to the state or district.
- Correspondence on each grant application, and local press coverage of awards can be added.
- These clippings, along with letters from grateful constituents, can serve as a source for favorable quotations.

Tracking Requests

- Monitor grant applications as they move through an agency's review process—develop contacts in agency congressional liaison offices or state or regional administering agencies.
- Maintain a follow-up calendar or log.
- Track all grants awarded in the district or state—even those your office did not work on.
- For sources that track federal funds by state, by county, and by congressional district, see the CRS Web page, *Tracking the Distribution of Federal Funds*, by Merete F. Gerli, at http://www.crs.gov/reference/general/geotracking.shtml. Contact the CRS author for search strategies and best sources.

Communicating with Staff

A weekly grants and projects report or letter is one way to keep both the Member and other staff fully informed of significant developments. This is particularly important for offices organized by functional responsibility.

- The report prepares the Member for the types of questions that may be asked during visits to the state or district and provides topics to be addressed in speeches.
- The legislative staff may benefit from knowing about pending state or local government actions that would have an impact on grants and projects. Conversely, grants and projects staff should also be able to rely on the legislative staff for information about pending bills that would alter or create federal programs or change relevant funding

levels. Sometimes, comments from constituents can supply data on whether programs are carrying out legislative intent and whether changes in agency regulations or legislation are needed. Such recommendations might then be the subject of congressional oversight hearings or might result in recommending changes in legislation.
- The press secretary should also be kept up to date on programs of interest in the district, so that current information can be presented in newsletters and press releases.

Assessing Constituent Requests

If a proposal or serious inquiry is submitted to a congressional office, an assessment of the stated problem should be made. First, this benefits the grant seeker, since any application for assistance will require that the problem be clearly stated and that the proposed solution provide some remedy. Secondly, this initial assessment can provide staff with a sense of direction: Are there other projects currently under way that address the problem? Is there already an appropriate federal or state program that is designed for such a project, or is the issue better addressed through local, state, or private organizations, or through legislation? Will the sought-after aid produce other problems for the community? What are its chances for success?

The initial review of the request should also involve an assessment of the applicant. A formal grant proposal will require an applicant to establish credibility. Individuals connected with a proposal might mention education, training, and professional credentials. Credibility for an organization may be established by giving its history, goals, activities, and primary accomplishments, as well as by letters of support, including by local governments. By reviewing such information, an office may avoid the hazard of offering support for a questionable applicant and may be in a better position to make decisions about support when several communities or organizations are applying for the same program—will all be treated equally or will support be given to selected applicants?

A written request from a constituent should always be acknowledged. If the request is a fairly common one, the office may be able to respond with a prepared packet of materials on available programs.

For large grants-in-aid projects, the congressional office may wish to contact the agency congressional liaison and ask to speak to a grants specialist for a particular program or funding need. This procedure is generally more time consuming for a congressional staffer than a simple referral, but it is often more informative. The agency may provide facts about budget levels, authorizations and appropriations, the amount of money available for the program, the total amount requested in applications on file, the number of applications received, and the number likely to be approved, agency priorities, categories of competition or targets by region, key dates and deadlines, and information on who makes recommendations and decisions.

If your constituent decides to submit a formal grant application for a particular program, the congressional office may recommend or arrange a meeting with agency offices in the district or state. Another way to get input from the agency early in the process is a pre-review of the application. Some agencies provide procedural review of proposals one or two months before the application deadline. Such a review, while not dealing with the substance of the proposal, allows an agency to inform the applicant of any technical problems or omissions to be corrected before the proposal is formally submitted.

When a constituent notifies the congressional office that a proposal has been submitted, the office can send a letter to the agency expressing the Member's interest in being kept informed of developments relating to the application. In addition, the letter may also request a list of all applicants for the particular grant from the Member's state or district. This enables the office to consider initiating letters of support from the Member to those applicants in his or her state or district who did not approach the office prior to submission of their application. Whether the Member chooses to support an applicant or extends support to all applicants from the state or district, the office should maintain contact with all interested parties as it is notified of progress reports from agency contacts.

Providing Information to Constituents

Cutbacks in federal programs mean many projects are made possible only through a combination of funding sources—federal and state government grants as well as private or corporate foundation grants should be considered. Grant seekers should know that most federal funding goes to states in the form of formula or block grants. For many programs, application for federal funds must be made through state administering agencies (SAAs). Whatever the funding source, it is important to emphasize that once a project has been clearly defined, constituents can improve their likelihood of success by doing preliminary research to find potential funding sources whose goals are most nearly consistent with their own.

Because the state, local, or private groups needing assistance may be unaware of available funding, or uncertain how to go about obtaining it, congressional offices can help identify sources. Congressional grants staff can also serve as liaison between grant seekers and government executive offices, including their own state offices that administer federal grants.

To assist Members in their representational duties, and to help congressional offices respond to grants questions, CRS has developed two Grants Web pages:

- For congressional staff, the *Grants, Business Opportunities, and Student Financial Aid* Web page, by Merete F. Gerli, focuses on key CRS reports and Internet products at *http://www.crs.gov/reference/general/WG02001.shtml*. It includes CRS publications on grants and programs that congressional offices can forward to their constituents; and a separate Web page of key sources (see next bullet) that Members may add to their home page for constituents.
- For grant seekers in districts and states, Members may add to their website the CRS *Grants and Federal Domestic Assistance* Web page, by Merete F. Gerli, see sample at http://www.crs.gov/reference/general/grants to provide useful information directly to constituents. It gives guidance and links to key Internet sources covering information readily available to the public. CRS automatically updates the Web page for Members on the House and Senate servers.

CRS also has a number of publications to help both congressional staff and grant seekers. Sources described cover key Internet sources and publications about federal and private funding. Constituents may search Internet sites from home computers or in local libraries, and can consult many of the published sources at public or university libraries or in government depository libraries in every state. Key useful CRS reports (in addition to the current report) to assist staff undertaking grants work include

- CRS Report RS21117, *Ethical Considerations in Assisting Constituents With Grant Requests Before Federal Agencies*, by Jack Maskell;

- CRS Report RL34012, *Resources for Grantseekers*, by Merete F. Gerli; and
- CRS Report RL32 159, *How to Develop and Write a Grant Proposal*, by Merete F. Gerli.

Some congressional offices may wish to help grant seekers by forwarding to them descriptions and contact information on federal grants programs for particular projects. The *Catalog of Federal Domestic Assistance* (CFDA) is available full text on the Internet. The site http://www.cfda.gov offers keyword searching, broad subject and recipient indexes, and listings by department, agency, and program title. The CFDA program descriptions also link to related websites such as federal department and agency home pages and Office of Management and Budget grants management circulars. Grant seekers themselves can then track notices of actual federal funding opportunities under CFDA programs at the website *Grants.gov* at http://www.grants.gov.

Congressional offices can also prepare their own information packets on federal grants programs, which are requested most frequently. Such packets could include program descriptions, brochures, the latest rules and regulations, changes in agency policy, application forms, and so on. For example, Members of rural states can become familiar with Department of Agriculture Rural Development programs; Members with urban constituencies and projects may want to consider Department of Housing and Urban Development programs.

Newsletters (print or e-mail) are a good way of reaching a large number of people. Some offices choose to send out either a special grants and projects newsletter or include a section on grants and projects in their regular newsletter. Subjects that could be developed include new programs, new appropriations, and descriptions of recently awarded grants.

A congressional office may occasionally choose to communicate with selected audiences through targeted mailings to inform constituents of the possible impact of new legislative or executive actions that might revise existing programs, create new ones, or alter funding levels; important dates and deadlines; and the advantages and limitations of various programs. This is especially important as new programs for are created and receive congressional appropriations: for example, a newly funded economic development program may be announced on *Grants.gov* with short application deadline, of which constituents should be made aware.

Another way to get information to interested constituents is for a congressional office to coordinate seminars on federal and private assistance at state and district locations. An office can sponsor programs bringing together federal, state, and local officials, as well as foundation, academic and corporate specialists, experienced volunteers, and constituents who share common concerns. Many agencies, foundations or the Foundation Center at http://www.fdncenter.org, and corporations are willing to provide speakers for district seminars arranged by congressional offices and also to provide such materials as brochures, sample proposals, and lists of information contacts. For telephone numbers to contact speakers from federal departments and agencies, congressional staff can use CRS Report 9 8-446, *Congressional Liaison Offices of Selected Federal Agencies*, by Audrey Crane-Hirsch. For constituent orientation and group seminars, Member may consider use of CRS products as handouts and presentation materials.

Although well-planned, balanced programs tailored to a particular audience can create good will, coordinating and following through on such seminars take a great deal of staff work and time. Such programs may also result in additional requests and demands on the sponsoring office.

PROPOSAL WRITING ASSISTANCE AND SOURCES

Although most offices do not write proposals, they are frequently approached by inexperienced constituents seeking guidance on what makes a good proposal. Offices aiding such constituents may find helpful CRS Report RL321 59, *How to Develop and Write a Grant Proposal*, by Merete F. Gerli, which discusses preliminary information gathering and preparation, developing ideas for the proposal, gathering community support, identifying funding resources, and seeking preliminary review of the proposal and support of relevant administrative officials. It also covers all aspects of writing the proposal, from outlining of project goals, stating the purpose and objectives of the proposal, explaining the program methods to solve the stated problem, and how the results of the project will be evaluated, to long-term project planning, and developing the proposal budget. The last section of the report lists free grants writing web sites, some in Spanish as well as English.

The Foundation Center and other organizations also publish guides to writing proposals; the Foundation Center offers a mini "Proposal Writing Course" on its website at *http://foundationcenter.org/getstarted/ tutorials/ shortcourse/index.html* and includes versions in Spanish, French, and other foreign languages. Constituents may also be advised that computer software templates can be found by searching the Internet under terms such as *grant proposal AND template*.

Congressional offices may wish to pass on the following suggestions.

- Allow sufficient time to prepare a thoroughly documented proposal, well before the application deadline. If possible, have someone outside the organization critique the proposal prior to submission.
- Follow the instructions given in the application form or in other material provided by the agency or foundation. Answer questions as asked.
- See that the proposal is clear and brief. Avoid jargon. Take pains to make the proposal interesting. Reviewing panels have limited time to devote to any single proposal. Whenever possible, fit the style of the proposal to the style of the agency or foundation being approached.
- When no form or instructions for submitting grant proposals are provided, the proposal should include the following:

1. a cover letter on the applicant's letterhead giving a brief description of the purpose and amount of the grant proposal, conveying the applicant's willingness to discuss the proposal in further detail
2. a half-page summary that includes identification of the applicant, the reasons for the request, proposed objectives and means to accomplish them, along with the total cost of the project, an indication of funds already obtained, and the amount being requested for this grant
3. an introduction in which the history, credentials, and accomplishments of the applicant are presented briefly (supporting documents can be included in an appendix)
4. a description of current conditions demonstrating the need for the proposed project
5. a statement of the project's objectives in specific, measurable terms
6. a description of the methods to be used to accomplish these objectives
7. a description of the means by which the project will be monitored and evaluated
8. a discussion of plans for continuing the project beyond the period covered by the grant
9. a detailed budget

WRITING LETTERS FOR GRANT SEEKERS

Constituents seeking funds for projects frequently ask congressional offices to write letters to federal departments and agencies on their behalf. CRS Report RS21117, *Ethical Considerations in Assisting Constituents With Grant Requests Before Federal Agencies*, by Jack Maskell, provides some guidance. Some grants, such as for firefighters and other funding for homeland security, are determined by formula to states and jurisdictions and letters may not be needed.

Explain to your constituent that the federal grants process is competitive, that your office can consider writing a letter to the department or agency once the individual submits a fully developed grant proposal. For most requests, use neutral language expressing the Member's "interest" in a proposal, rather than "support." Lending "support" to a proposal that might not be funded under the competitive process (and when there are competing applications from several constituents) might lead to disappointment and reflect negatively on the Member.

For most constituent requests, write a letter only when your constituent is ready to submit the grant proposal to the department or agency.

- Information needed from the grant seeker:
    - name of applicant; contact person for the project if different
    - grant program name and number
    - agency contact address, grants officer's name if available
    - deadline for proposal submission
    - project name and summary
- The project summary should highlight:
    - what the project/program does and who it serves
    - why this program is important to the community
    - any unique features of the project, needs not already being met
    - other support for the project such as local government
    - specifically how the grant money will be used
- Write directly to the person in the department of agency; provide a copy of the letter to your constituent to submit with the proposal.
- The Member's letter could say why this is important to his district, what needs are being met, etc.—the summary supplied by the constituent should give the objectives of the proposal/project.

- Close by asking the grants officer to let the Member know when a decision will be made; and to keep your office informed about the progress of the proposal.

A sample letter of support, written on the Member or Senator's letterhead, might read as follows:

> Ms. Ronda Mason, Acting Administrator
> Office of Juvenile Justice and Delinquency Prevention
> 810 Seventh Street N.W.
> Washington, DC 20531
>
> Dear Ms. Mason,
>
> I am writing to express my support for the Local Youth Mentoring Initiative grant application submitted by a coalition of Big Brothers Big Sisters (BBBS) affiliates from across the state to expand their mentoring programs for at-risk youth.
>
> The three coalition member groups have been working with families in our state for more than forty years. Each of the affiliates currently serves between 350 and 500 children, matching each young person with a professionally supported mentor. Since 2000, the state's BBS agencies have expanded their program offerings. With the support of grants from the U.S. Departments of Education and Health and Human Services, they now serve the children of prisoners and children in afterschool and in-school sites.
>
> This funding will allow the coalition to offer mentoring programs to 500 more at-risk youth in the state, including those in foster care. Each agency already has more than 100 children currently on waiting lists and all are ready to expand their pgrograms as soon as new resources become available
>
> I am proud to support programs to improve the criminal justice system, assist victims of crime and support youth mentoring. Office of Juvenile Justice and Delinquency Prevention studies have documented that mentoring leads to significant reductions in illegal drug and alcohol use, truancy and aggressive behavior, as well as improvemens in confidence and school performance. In the midst of this economic recession the good work of organizations like Big Brothers Big Sisters is critical to maintaining the strength of families and communities.

> I fully support the BBS coalition's application and urge your serious consideration of this worthy project. If you have any questions, please contact my Grants Coordinator, Natalie Keegan, at (202) 555-1212.
>
> Sincerely,
>
> Mike Firestone
> United States Member of Congress

ANNOUNCING GRANTS AWARDS

Although there is some variation, the usual announcement procedure in cases of allocated federal funds is for the agency making the award to notify the Senate office first (a Senator of the President's party may be first notified), then the House office, and finally the recipient. This allows Members of Congress an opportunity to notify recipients of grants. Not all awards are announced publicly. In the case of block grants, the Office of Management and Budget notifies Senate offices of the allocations among the states. The state's decision on how to distribute funds among local communities is, however, not necessarily communicated to congressional offices. In these cases, a good state agency contact may be willing to provide the office with this information. Announcements of grants awarded are often posted on Member Web pages.

Many congressional offices develop files or databases of grants awarded to track funding to their districts and states. Detailed information is difficult to obtain. P.L. 109-282, the Federal Funding Accountability and Transparency Act of 2006, called for the Office of Management and Budget (OMB) to develop a database, which became USAspending.gov. For a summary of sources and limitations of currently available data, and the new law's requirements, see CRS Web page, *Tracking the Distribution of Federal Funds*, by Merete F. Gerli, at http://www.crs.gov/reference/general/geotracking.shtml. Contact the CRS author for search strategies and best sources.

To avoid disappointment, congressional staff might consider cautioning grant seekers from making requests that are unlikely to be approved at the federal level. Suggest considering other funding sources early in the process. In cases where grant applications are made and turned down, the congressional office may notify constituents of their right to know why the award was not granted and what the appeals process is. Constituents may ask the agency for an analysis of the strengths and weaknesses of the proposal, or may give the agency permission to provide the congressional office with this information. Alternative programs or other approaches may be suggested following an adverse decision. The constituent might also decide to improve the initial application and start the process again.

FEDERAL ASSISTANCE AND SOURCES

Hundreds of grants or loans for various purposes are available from federal departments and agencies. Most federal funding (over 90%) goes to state and local governments that determine state and local needs, and that themselves offer competitive grants and funding opportunities. New programs and federal funding to enhance homeland security or enhance emergency services are of particular interest to many local jurisdictions. Other federal funds not dispensed through grants, but much sought after, are used for defense procurement, construction of federal installations, or infrastructure (e.g., military bases, federal office buildings, and federal projects such as flood control and highway construction). Congressional offices can assist state and local governments, non-profit organizations, and other grant seekers become aware of available funds and how to go about obtaining them.

Staff members can contact federal agencies to find agency interest in certain projects; relay the findings to those interested and qualified for assistance in their states and districts; and notify home state governments, organizations, businesses, and people of what funds are available.

Once a grant application is filed, offices frequently keep in touch with agencies. Contact can be maintained by letter, phone, e-mail, or in person as the situation dictates. Concerted action on the part of the staff may result in more federal funds being spent in a state or district, thereby providing greater benefit to the constituency.

Federal program and contact information is given in the *Catalog of Federal Domestic Assistance* (CFDA), at http://www.cfda.gov. Current notices of grant opportunities appear on the website *Grants.gov* at http://www.grants. See sections below for more information about these key sources.

Federal Grants and the Appropriations Process

Congress may also designate or "earmark" federal funds for projects in districts and states in annual appropriations legislation. Because much of the annual U.S. budget consists of expenditures for entitlement programs such as Social Security, mandatory spending through authorizing legislation and interest payments, or allocations in the form of formula and block grants to states and local governments, discretionary funding for new grant awards is limited. The appropriations measure that a congressional office chooses to submit often reflects the Member's legislative agenda as well as the needs of the state or district.

Grant seekers who wish to ask support of their Senator or Representative for project funding should consider the congressional budget process calendar. Appropriations measures for the next fiscal year (October 1-September 30) are usually submitted as early as February.

If congressionally directed spending seems appropriate, applicants may be asked by the Member to make a formal request accompanied by supporting materials, including

- project description
- research and documentation of the need for the project (such as a feasibility study and history of community support)
- letters of support from elected officials and local community leaders
- amount requested, anticipated total project cost, sources of other funding (state, private, local match), and any history of past funding

Grant seekers may contact both Representatives and Senators about their project. Although an "earmark" may appear in either a House or Senate committee report, a conference committee (composed of an equal number of House and Senate members) makes the final decisions on funding. Having support of both Representative and Senator(s) for a project may enhance a grant seeker's success for an "earmark."

The congressional appropriations process follows an annual time line, beginning in February of each year. Grant seekers such as state and local governments or nonprofit organizations can submit requests for project support and funding to Representatives and Senators before the beginning of the budget cycle.

- February: The President submits to Congress the proposed Budget of the United States.
- Members submit requests for discretionary funding on behalf of projects in their districts or states prior to the start of appropriations hearings in early March.
- Early March: The House Appropriations Committee's 12 subcommittees begin hearings on proposed spending bills.
- May - August: The House votes on appropriations bills beginning in May and tries to finish before the end of the fiscal year, September 30. The Senate generally follows the House in considering appropriations measures. In recent years, voting has continued into the fall, and continuing resolutions are passed to ensure that federal offices and programs do not close down.
- After each chamber votes on its version of an appropriations bill, a conference committee, consisting of equal numbers of House and Senate members, meets to reconcile any differences and makes final decisions on spending.
- Funding for district and state projects included in both House and Senate appropriations bills will generally be approved by the conferees, and submitted for floor vote by the full House and Senate.
- After approval, appropriations bills are forwarded to the President for signature.
- Members notify grant seekers of projects successfully funded.

Types of Federal Assistance

Currently, programs in the *Catalog of Federal Domestic Assistance* (CFDA), the key source to federal program information (see below), are classified into several types of financial and nonfinancial assistance. For a fuller explanation of these categories, see the CFDA program descriptions themselves.

Grants

Grants are generally considered desirable by applicants since they are an outright award of funds.

- **Formula Grants:** allocations of money to states or their subdivisions for activities of a continuing nature not confined to a specific project. Includes block grants to states and local governments.

- **Project Grants:** funding, for fixed or known periods, of specific projects or the delivery of specific services or products, including fellowships, scholarships, research grants, training grants, traineeships, experimental and demonstration grants, evaluation grants, planning grants, technical assistance grants, survey grants, construction grants, and unsolicited contractual agreements. Can also be referred to as discretionary or categorical grants or funding.

- **Direct Payments for Specified Use:** federal financial assistance provided directly to individuals, private firms, and other private institutions to encourage or subsidize a particular activity.

- **Direct Payments with Unrestricted Use:** federal financial assistance provided directly to beneficiaries who satisfy federal eligibility requirements with no restrictions as to how the money is spent.

Loans

Because loans must be repaid, they are often viewed by applicants as less desirable than grants. However, with the reduction of federal funds available for grants and the increasing level of competition for such funds, loans are often the only form of assistance available.

- **Direct Loans:** lending of federal funds for a specific period of times, with a reasonable expectation of repayment; may or may not require the payment of interest.

- **Guaranteed/Insured Loans:** programs in which the federal government makes an arrangement to indemnify a lender against part or all of any defaults by those responsible for repayment of loans.

Insurance

Some federal programs provide financial assistance to assure reimbursement for losses sustained under specified conditions. Coverage may be provided directly by the federal government or through private carriers and may or may not require the payment of premiums.

Goods and Properties

The federal government has programs both for the sale, exchange, or donation of property and for temporary use or loan of goods and property.

- **Sale, Exchange, or Donation of Property and Goods:** programs which provide for the sale, exchange, or donation of federal real property, personal property, commodities, and other goods including land, buildings, equipment, food, and drugs.

- **Use of Property, Facilities, and Equipment:** programs which provide for the loan of, use of, or access to federal facilities or property wherein the federally- owned facilities or property do not remain in the possession of the recipient of the assistance.

Services, Information, Training, and Employment

The federal government offers a variety of programs to assist communities and citizens.

- **Provision of Specialized Services:** programs which provide federal personnel to directly perform certain tasks for the benefit of communities or individuals.

- **Advisory Services and Counseling:** programs which provide federal specialists to consult, advise, or counsel communities or individuals, to include conferences, workshops, or personal contacts.

- **Dissemination of Technical Information:** programs which provide for the publication and distribution of information or data of a specialized technical nature frequently through clearinghouses or libraries.

- **Training:** programs which provide instructional activities conducted directly by a federal agency for individuals not employed by the federal government.

- **Investigation of Complaints:** federal administrative agency activities that are initiated in response to requests, either formal or informal, to examine or investigate claims of violations of federal statutes, policy, or procedure.

- **Federal Employment:** programs which reflect the government-wide responsibilities of the Office of Personnel Management in the recruitment and hiring of federal civilian agency personnel.

CATALOG OF FEDERAL DOMESTIC ASSISTANCE

The key sources of information about federal programs, projects, services, and activities that provide assistance or benefits to the public are the *Catalog of Federal Domestic Assistance* (CFDA) and *Grants.gov*. The *Catalog*, produced by the General Services Administration (GSA) and searchable for free on the Internet at http://www.cfda.gov, describes some 1,600 authorized financial and nonfinancial assistance programs of federal departments and agencies.

About 1,000 CFDA programs are grants. For grants programs, funding notices and application information appear in notices of current funding opportunities posted at *Grants.gov* at http://www.grants.gov.

CFDA program descriptions include the following:

- federal agency administering a program
- legislation authorizing the program
- objectives and goals of program
- types of financial or nonfinancial assistance provided
- uses and restrictions
- eligibility requirements
- application and award process
- criteria for selecting proposals
- amount of obligations for the past, current, and estimates for future fiscal years
- funding caps and range of awards
- regulations, guidelines, and literature relevant to a program
- information contacts and headquarters, regional, and local offices
- related programs
- examples of funded projects
- formula and matching requirements, where applicable
- requirements for post-assistance reports

Updated information on federal programs also appears in the daily *Federal Register*, http://www.gpoaccess.gov/fr/index.html. Federal departments and agencies may also provide information and guidelines for specific programs on their websites. These websites may also provide a list of grantees from the previous fiscal year and indicate the amount of money still available for the coming year.

Congressional staff may suggest that constituents seeking federal funding search CFDA themselves by subject, keyword, beneficiary and other options for identifying appropriate program information.

Some congressional offices may wish to forward to constituents a preliminary CFDA search of potential federal funding. Descriptions of programs identified will have to be carefully analyzed by grant seekers themselves to see whether they may be appropriate. Early in the process, the grant seeker should contact the department or agency indicated in the CFDA program description for latest information on funding availability, program requirements, and deadlines. Often a referral to a local or state office will be given. Many may be project or formula (block) grants to states that in turn accept grants applications and determine award recipients.

GRANTS.GOV

As part of the federal government's e-grants initiative, federal departments and agencies are required to post grants opportunities notices on *Grants.gov* at http://www.grants.gov. *Grants.gov* posts funding notices from more than 1,000 federal grant programs and provides a uniform application process for all federal grants opportunities. Beginning in 2009, some federal departments and agencies allow application through their own or other websites, such as FedConnect at https://www.fedconnect.net/Fedconnect/. *Grants.gov* notices link and direct grantseekers to these other websites.

Except for familiarizing themselves with information provided on the *Grants.gov* site, and sometimes posting *Grants.gov* funding notices on Member websites if they wish, congressional staff generally need not search this website for funding opportunities for constituents. CRS grants websites and reports include *Grants.gov*, which is free to the public, as a key source for grant seekers themselves to access and search.

Registration by the grant seeker who will be making the application is required at *Grants.gov*. Before applying, grant seekers must also obtain Dun and Bradstreet (DUNS) and Central Contractor Registration (CCR) numbers. *Grants.gov* includes instructions.

For grant seekers who have identified appropriate federal funding programs (through CFDA or department and agency websites), *Grants.gov* enables them to

- search for current funding opportunity notices (including by CFDA program number);
- sign up for e-mail notification of future grant opportunities;
- download grants application packages and instructions or go to another website to apply;
- submit applications electronically through a uniform process for all federal grant- making agencies; and
- track the progress of their applications using unqieu IDs and passwords.

For questions about *Grants.gov*, congressional staff can call the *Grants.gov* program office at (202) 205-1154. The managing federal agency for the program is the Department of Health and Human Services, the federal government's largest grant-making department.

AMERICAN RECOVERY AND REINVESTMENT ACT (ARRA)

The American Recovery and Reinvestment Act (ARRA , P.L. 111-5) provides $787 billion through a vast array of discretionary and mandatory spending and tax provisions. Additional funding is provided for existing and some new programs. Funds are distributed to states, localities, other entities and individuals through a combination of formula and competitive grants and direct assistance. The following websites provide program, agency, and state information:

- **Recovery.gov,** http://www.recovery The Administration's website covering implementation and oversight of the stimulus. It currently includes overview information about the legislation, a timeline for implementation, a frequently asked questions page, and an announcement page that will be regularly updated.

- **Agency Recovery Sites,** http://www.recovery Links to information about federal agency and department programs.

- **State Recovery Sites,** http://www.recovery. Covers state projects and state contacts for grants programs.

- **United States Conference of Mayors,** http://www.usmayors.org/recovery Gives *State Breakdown of ARRA*, http://www.usmayors.org/recovery/documents/report-stateprog.pdf, and *Key Program Summaries*, http://www.usmayors.org/recovery/documents/program-summaries.xlsx.

DEVELOPING FEDERAL AND STATE GRANTS CONTACTS

Many federal agencies have a number of offices: a central office in Washington, DC; a series of regional and state offices; and, in some cases, local or area offices. Each program in the CFDA includes information contacts, either giving the name, address, and telephone number of the main program officer, or referring applicants to the regional, state, or local office of the agency. Federal Regional Agency Offices are given in CFDA at https://www.cfda.gov/index?s=appendix list&tab=list.

Congressional offices can channel their requests for program funding information and get help identifying appropriate grants officers through federal department and agency congressional liaison offices (see CRS Report 9 8-446, *Congressional Liaison Offices of Selected Federal Agencies*, by Audrey Celeste Crane-Hirsch for telephone numbers). Establishing a good relationship with program grants officers is usually beneficial—they are normally well informed and willing to share information with congressional grants and projects staff. The liaison office may also be willing to brief congressional staff so that they may become more familiar with the way the agency is organized and where responsibilities are assigned, as well as with published materials that may be available on various programs.

State and district grants and projects staff usually work closely with federal agency representatives in their areas, with their state Members of Congress and Senators, with state and local elected officials, and with state councils of government. Many federal programs are administered directly by state agencies or other entities within the state, and many states have programs funded out of their own appropriations that supplement or complement federal programs. Local councils of government, where they exist, have access to federal funds for providing technical assistance, guidance, and counseling in the grants process. Constituents are, as a rule, best served by being put in touch with program officers closest to them as early as possible.

Some congressional grants and projects veterans report that a congressional office that encourages cooperation among local organizations, foundations, units of government, and councils of government can serve as a catalyst for applicants by improving communications, which may in turn enhance the chances for proposal approval. When congressional staff take the time to express appreciation for assistance provided by federal personnel, foundation officials, and others involved in the grants process, they may possibly improve their chances for future assistance.

ROLE OF STATE ADMINISTERING AGENCIES (SAAS) AND CONTACTS

Many federal grants such as formula and block grants, and now economic stimulus allocations, are awarded directly to state governments, which then set priorities and allocate funds within that state. To help constituents, congressional grants staff need to learn their SAAs, the state counterpart offices accepting grants applications and disbursing federal formula and other grants. For more information on how a state intends to distribute formula grant funds, grant seekers need to contact the state administering agency.

Many federal department and agency websites provide state contacts. Often the site will have an interactive U.S. map where grant seekers can click on their state and obtain program and funding contact information. State government agencies provide coordination of local efforts to obtain federal funds through grant programs that are already allocated to the state; and state government agencies are familiar with federal program requirements, can assist with proposals, and can provide other guidance. In fact, many federal grant programs require that an applicant complete a pre-application screening at the state level before submitting requests.

- Federal congressional liaison offices can help congressional staff identify SAAs for their programs: use CRS Report 98-446,

Congressional Liaison Offices of Selected Federal Agencies, by Audrey Celeste Crane-Hirsch.
- Many states require federal grants applicant to submit a copy of their application for state government-level review and comment, and have designated a 'Single Point of Contact' under Executive Order 12372, listed by Office of Management and Budget (OMB) at http://www.whitehouse.gov/omb/grants/spoc.html. The State offices listed here coordinate government (both federal and state) grants development and may provide guidance to grant seekers.
- Other state government agency websites may be identified at the federal government site USA, State and Local Agencies by Topic at http://www.usa.gov/Agencies/State_and_Territories/Agencies_by_Topic.shtml.
- Federal department and agency regional, state, and local offices which grant seekers should contact early in their proposal development are given in the CFDA's list of Regional Agency Offices at https://www.cfda.gov/index?s= appendix&mode=list&tab=list.

Many federal department and agency websites include SAAs and often the site will have an interactive U.S. map. Grant seekers can click on their state and obtain program and state contact information. A selection of some executive department websites includes the following:[1]

- Agriculture Rural Development State Contacts
  http://www.rurdev.usda.gov/recd_map.html
- National Endowment for the Arts (NEA) Partners
  http://www.arts.gov/partner/state/SAA_RAO_list.html
- Commerce Offices and Services
  http://www.commerce
- Education (ED) State Contacts
  http://www.ed.gov/about/contacts/state/index.html
- Energy (DOE) State Contacts
  http://www.eere.energy
- Environmental Protection Agency (EPA) Grant Regional Office
  http://www.epa.gov/ogd/grants
- Federal Emergency Management Agency (FEMA) State Offices and Agencies http://www.fema.gov/about/contact/statedr.shtm

Grants Work in a Congressional Office

- Health and Human Services (HHS), Administration on Children and Families: State Contacts http://www.acf.hhs.gov/acf_contact_us.html#state
- Homeland Security (DHS) State Contacts and Grant Award Information http://www.dhs.gov/xgovt/grants
- Housing and Urban Development (HUD) State/Local Offices http://www.hud.gov/localoffices.cfm
- National Endowment for the Humanities (NEA) State Councils http://www.neh.gov/whoweare/statecouncils.html
- Office of Justice Programs (OJP) State Administering Agencies http://www.ojp.usdoj.gov/saa/
- Labor (DOL) Education and Training Administration, State Contacts http://www.doleta.gov/regions/statecontacts/
- Small Business Administration http://www.sba.gov/localresources/index.html
- Transportation, Federal Transit Administration (FTA) Regional Offices http://www.fta.dot.gov/regional
- Veterans Affairs State/Territory Offices http://www.va.gov/statedva.htm

FOUNDATIONS AND CORPORATE GRANTS

With reductions in federal programs, congressional grants specialists may wish to suggest other funding possibilities to their constituents as alternatives or supplements to federal grants. Private foundation funding can be used for federal grants that have matching requirements.

Small local projects should begin their search for help at the community level from local businesses or institutions. Support may be available in the form of cash contributions or in-kind contributions of property, buildings, equipment, or professional expertise. Evidence of such community-based support may strengthen a federal grant proposal.

Grant making foundations are established for the express purpose of providing funds for projects in their areas of interest, and all must comply with specific Internal Revenue Service regulations to maintain their tax-exempt status. Every year, each is required to give away money equal to at least 5% of the market value of its assets, and each must make its tax records public.

Although there are all kinds of foundation and corporate grants available, competition for these funds is great, and, just as is the case in searching for federal support, grant seekers enhance their chances for success by doing preliminary research to find grant makers whose priorities and goals match their own. By searching foundation websites, grant seekers can find guidelines, copies of annual reports and tax returns to learn whether their proposals match a foundation's areas of interest and geographic guidelines; whether the proposal is within its budgetary constraints; and whether it normally funds the type of project being considered.

There are many different kinds of foundations, with widely varying resources and purposes. Some are national in scope; others are set up purely for the purpose of local giving. Some are endowed by an individual or family to provide funds for specific social, educational, or religious purposes; others are company-sponsored; still others are publicly supported community foundations. Grant seekers might begin by identifying state or local foundations. These may have a greater interest in local projects than larger foundations mainly concerned with programs of national significance. Direct corporate giving should also be explored: many corporations support local projects in areas where they have their headquarters or plants, or sponsor projects which somehow enhance their corporate image.

Because of this variety, different strategies may be needed for dealing with different foundations. A few foundations publicize their funding policies, and even initiate projects, but generally they do not. Usually, the grant seeker must take the first step and approach the foundation about his or her proposal. Although it is hard to generalize about foundations, they tend to be more flexible than federal funding agencies and to have fewer bureaucratic requirements. Many foundations see their purpose as providing short-term, startup funding for demonstration projects. Frequently, such foundations are the best source to turn to for funding emergency situations or small, high- risk, innovative programs. In some cases, foundation officials will work closely with inexperienced grant seekers to help them develop realistic proposals.

The Foundation Center serves as a clearinghouse of information on private philanthropic giving and is a good starting point for identifying likely funding sources. The center's office in Washington, DC, can advise staff on other sources of private funding. The Foundation Center can be contacted via phone at (202) 331-1400. The center's website, http://www.foundationcenter.org, includes extensive information about private funders; posts requests for proposals (RFPs) for funding opportunities from foundations in all subject fields; offers Web and in-person training, many of them free, including a

"Proposal Writing Short Course;" and produces a number of directories and guides to private and corporate funding sources, in print, CD-ROM, Web, and other electronic formats. The Foundation Center also posts IRS Form 990 for nonprofit organizations at http://foundationcenter.org/findfunders/990finder/.

In addition to its major reference collections in New York, Washington, DC, Cleveland, and San Francisco, the Foundation Center maintains a national network of cooperating library collections in each state, with print and electronic resources available free to the public. Addresses of these library collections are provided on the Foundation Center website at http://foundationcenter.org/ collections. At these libraries, grant seekers may search the *Foundation Directory Online* by field of interest, by foundation location, and other categories to produce lists of likely funding sources for grant seekers. For congressional staff, the Library of Congress maintains a subscription to the *Foundation Directory Online*.

Other websites that provide free listings of foundations include the Council on Foundations Web page, Community Foundations by State, at http://classic.cof.org/locator/; and the Grantsmanship Center's Funding Sources, which for each state lists "top," corporate, and community foundations, at http://tgci.com/funding. Congressional offices may wish to send constituents state listings from these websites.

USEFUL SOURCES OF GRANTS INFORMATION

CRS Grants Web Pages

Grants, Business Opportunities, and Student Financial Aid, by Merete F. Gerli http://www.crs.gov/reference/general/WG02001.shtml
Focuses on CRS grants Web products and publications. CRS reports provide guidance to congressional staff on federal programs and funding; and may be forwarded to constituents in response to grants requests.

Grants and Federal Domestic Assistance, by Merete F. Gerli
http://www.crs.gov/reference/general/grants
Provides Internet links to free key federal and private grants and funding information, including the *Catalog of Federal Domestic Assistance*, *Grants.gov*, and other federal websites; and the Foundation Center, and other private funding resources. Members may add this CRS Web page to their

home page so grant seekers in districts and states can access Web information directly using the Member's home page as portal to key grants sources.

Additional Federal Sources

For Catalog of Federal Domestic Assistance and Grants.gov, see sections of this chapter and the CRS websites described above.

A-Z Index of U.S. Government Departments and Agencies (General Services Administration) http://www.usa.gov/Agencies/Federal/All_Agencies/index.shtml To better develop a grant proposal, search a department or agency's homepage to learn more about its programs and objectives. The website USA at http://www.usa.gov also includes *Government Benefits, Grants and Financial Aid* for citizens http://www.usa.gov/Citizen/Topics/Benefits.shtml;

Government-to-Government
http://www.usa.gov/Government/State_Local/Grants.shtml

Thousands of grants and loans are made by the federal government to state and local governments and other public entities. This site provides one-stop access to grants management and federal assistance programs, in addition to resources about acquisition and procurement, financial management, and taxes;

Grants, Loans, and Other Assistance for nonprofit organizations http://www.usa.gov/ Business/Nonprofit.shtml links to federal department and agency information and service, including fundraising and outreach, grants, loans and other assistance, laws and regulations, management and operations, registration and licensing, and tax information;

Information by Topic for Business provides financial assistance information for small business, government contractors, and foreign business in the United States.

http://www.usa.gov/Business/Business_Gateway.shtml;

Grants Management Circulars (Office of Management and Budget) http://www.whitehouse.gov/omb/grants

OMB establishes government-wide grants management policies and guidelines through circulars and common rules. OMB Circulars are cited in CFDA program descriptions and may be printed out in full-text.

Other Resources

Grants and Related Resources (Michigan State University Libraries)
http://www.lib.msu.edu/harris23/grants
The site provides government and private grants resources, primarily Internet, by subject or group categories, and is updated frequently. Subpages include

Funding for Business and Economic Development
http://www.lib.msu.edu/harris23/grants
Grants for Nonprofit
http://www.lib.msu.edu/harris23/grants
Grants for Individuals (primarily financial aid and scholarships)
http://www.lib.msu.edu/harris23/grants

End Notes

[1] Compiled by CRS from executive department and agency websites.

In: A Government Guide to Grants
Editors: Nathan E. Legaspi

ISBN: 978-1-60876-751-9
© 2010 Nova Science Publishers, Inc.

Chapter 3

HOW TO DEVELOP AND WRITE A GRANT

Merete F. Gerli

SUMMARY

This chapter is intended for Members and staff assisting grant seekers in districts and states and covers writing proposals for both government and private foundations grants. In preparation for writing a proposal, the report first discusses preliminary information gathering and preparation, developing ideas for the proposal, gathering community support, identifying funding resources, and seeking preliminary review of the proposal and support of relevant administrative officials.

The second section of the report covers the actual writing of the proposal, from outlining of project goals, stating the purpose and objectives of the proposal, explaining the program methods to solve the stated problem, and how the results of the project will be evaluated, to long-term project planning, and, finally, developing the proposal budget.

The last section of the report provides a listing of free grants-writing websites, including guidelines from the Catalog of Federal Domestic Assistance and the Foundation Center's "Proposal Writing Short Course."

Related CRS reports are CRS Report RL34035, *Grants Work in a Congressional Office*, by Merete F. Gerli; CRS Report RL34012, *Resources for Grantseekers*, by Merete F. Gerli; and CRS Report RS21 117, *Ethical*

Considerations in Assisting Constituents With Grant Requests Before Federal Agencies, by Jack Maskell.

DEVELOPING A GRANT PROPOSAL

Preparation

A well-formed grant proposal is one that is carefully prepared, thoughtfully planned, and concisely packaged. The potential applicant generally seeks first to become familiar with all of the pertinent program criteria of the funding institution. Before developing a proposal, the potential applicant may refer to the information contact listed in the agency or foundation program description to learn whether funding is available, when applicable deadlines occur, and the process used by the grantor agency or private foundation for accepting applications.

Grant seekers should know that the basic requirements, application forms, information, and procedures vary among grant-making agencies and foundations. Federal agencies and large foundations may have formal application packets, strict guidelines, and fixed deadlines with which applicants must comply, while smaller foundations may operate more informally and even provide assistance to inexperienced grantseekers. However, the steps outlined in this chapter generally apply to any grant-seeking effort.

Individuals without prior grant proposal writing experience may find it useful to attend a grantsmanship class or workshop. Applicants interested in locating workshops or consulting more resources on grantsmanship and proposal development should consult the Internet sites listed at the end of this chapter and explore other resources in their local libraries.

Local governments may obtain grant writing assistance from a state's office of Council of Governments (CSG) or Regional Council. The primary mission of CSG is to promote and strengthen state government in the federal system by providing staff services to organizations of state officials. Grassroots or small faith-based nonprofit organizations can seek the help and advice of larger more seasoned nonprofit organizations or foundations in their state.

Developing Ideas for the Proposal

The first step in proposal planning is the development of a clear, concise description of the proposed project. To develop a convincing proposal for project funding, the project must fit into the philosophy and mission of the grant-seeking organization or agency; and the need that the proposal is addressing must be well documented and well-articulated. Typically, funding agencies or foundations will want to know that a proposed activity or project reinforces the overall mission of an organization or grant seeker, and that the project is necessary. To make a compelling case, the following should be included in the proposal:

- Nature of the project, its goals, needs, and anticipated outcomes;
- How the project will be conducted;
- Timetable for completion;
- How best to evaluate the results (performance measures);
- Staffing needs, including use of existing staff and new hires or volunteers; and
- Preliminary budget, covering expenses and financial requirements, to determine what funding levels to seek.

When developing an idea for a proposal, it is also important to determine if the idea has already been considered in the applicant's locality or state. A thorough check should be made with state legislators, local government, and related public and private agencies which may currently have grant awards or contracts to do similar work. If a similar program already exists, the applicant may need to reconsider submitting the proposed project, particularly if duplication of effort is perceived. However, if significant differences or improvements in the proposed project's goals can be clearly established, it may be worthwhile to pursue federal or private foundation assistance.

Community Support

For many proposals, community support is essential. Once a proposal summary is developed, an applicant may look for individuals or groups representing academic, political, professional, and lay organizations which may be willing to support the proposal in writing. The type and caliber of community support is critical in the initial and subsequent review phases. Numerous letters of support can influence the administering agency or foundation. An applicant may elicit support from local government agencies and public officials. Letters of endorsement detailing exact areas of project sanction and financial or in-kind commitment are often requested as part of a proposal to a federal agency. Several months may be required to develop letters of endorsement since something of value (e.g., buildings, staff, services) is sometimes negotiated between the parties involved. Note that letters from Members of Congress may be requested once a proposal has been fully developed and is ready for submission.

While money is the primary concern of most grantseekers, thought should be given to the kinds of nonmonetary contributions that may be available. In many instances, academic institutions, corporations, and other nonprofit groups in the community may be willing to contribute technical and professional assistance, equipment, or space to a worthy project. Not only can such contributions reduce the amount of money being sought, but evidence of such local support is often viewed favorably by most grant-making agencies or foundations.

Many agencies require, in writing, affiliation agreements (a mutual agreement to share services between agencies) and building space commitments prior to either grant approval or award. Two useful methods of generating community support may be to form a citizen advisory committee or to hold meetings with community leaders who would be concerned with the subject matter of the proposal. The forum may include the following:

- Discussion of the merits of the proposal,
- Development of a strategy to create proposal support from a large number of community groups, institutions, and organizations, and
- Generation of data in support of the proposal.

Identifying Funding Resources

Once the project has been specifically defined, the grant seeker needs to research appropriate funding sources. Both the applicant and the grantor agency or foundation should have the same interests, intentions, and needs if a proposal is to be considered an acceptable candidate for funding. It is generally not productive to send out proposals indiscriminately in the hope of attracting funding. Grant-making agencies and foundations whose interest and intentions are consistent with those of the applicant are the most likely to provide support. An applicant may cast a wide, but targeted, net. Many projects may only be accomplished with funds coming from a combination of sources, among them federal, state, or local programs and grants from private or corporate foundations.

The best funding resources are now largely on the Internet. Key sources for funding information include the federal government's *Catalog of Federal Domestic Assistance* (CFDA), http://www.cfda.gov, and the Foundation Center, http://www.foundationcenter.org, the clearinghouse of private and corporate foundation funding. For a summary of federal programs and sources, see CRS Report RL34012, *Resources for Grantseekers*, by Merete F. Gerli, and other CRS reports on topics such as community or social services block grants to states, rural development assistance, federal allocations for homeland security, and other funding areas, may be requested from a Senator or Representative.

A review of the government or private foundation's program descriptions' objectives and uses, as well as any use restrictions, can clarify which programs might provide funding for an idea. When reviewing individual CFDA program descriptions, applicants may also target the related programs as potential resources. Also, the kinds of projects the agency or foundation funded in the past may be helpful in fashioning your grant proposal. Program listings in the CFDA or foundation information will often include examples of past funded projects.

Many federal grants do not go directly to the final beneficiary, but are awarded through "block" or "formula" grants to state or local agencies which, in turn, distribute the funds. For more information, CRS Report R40486, *Block Grants: Perspectives and Controversies*, by Robert Jay Dilger and Eugene Boyd, and CRS Report RL30705, *Federal Grants to State and Local Governments: A Brief History*, by Natalie Keegan, may be requested from a Representative or Senator.

There are many types of foundations: national, family, community, corporate, etc. For district or community projects, as a general rule, it is a good idea to look for funding sources close to home, which are frequently most concerned with solving local problems. Corporations, for example, tend to support projects in areas where they have offices or plants. Most foundations only provide grants to nonprofit organizations (those registered by the Internal Revenue Service as having 501(c) tax-exempt status), though the Foundation Center publishes information about foundation grants to individuals.

Once a potential grantor agency or foundation is identified, an applicant may contact it and ask for a grant application kit or information. Federal agencies may refer applicants to the website Grants.gov. Later, the grant seeker may ask some of the grantor agency or foundation personnel for suggestions, criticisms, and advice about the proposed project. In many cases, the more agency or foundation personnel know about the proposal, the better the chance of support and of an eventual favorable decision.

Federal agencies are required to report funding information as funds are approved, increased, or decreased among projects within a given state depending on the type of required reporting. Also, grant seekers may consider reviewing the federal budget for the current and future fiscal years to determine proposed dollar amounts for particular budget functions.

The grant seeker should carefully study the eligibility requirements for each government or foundation program under consideration (see for example the Applicant Eligibility and Rules and Regulations sections of the CFDA program description). Federal department and agency websites generally include additional information about their programs. CFDA program descriptions and websites include information contacts. Applicants should direct questions and seek clarification about requirements and deadlines from the contacts. The applicant may learn that he or she is required to provide services otherwise unintended such as a service to particular client groups, or involvement of specific institutions. It may necessitate the modification of the original concept in order for the project to be eligible for funding. Questions about eligibility should be discussed with the appropriate program officer.

For federal grants, funding opportunities notices appear on the website Grants.gov at http://www.grants.gov. Applicants can search and sign up for email notification of funding opportunities, and download applications packages. To submit applications, registration is required. The grantseeker must also obtain Dun and Bradstreet (DUNS) and Central Contractor Registration (CCR) numbers before registering: Grants.gov provides instructions and links. Deadlines for submitting applications are often not negotiable, though some federal programs do have open application dates (refer to the CFDA program description). For private foundation funding opportunities, grant seekers should contact foundations or check the Foundation Center's website for daily postings of Requests for Proposals (RFPs) at http://foundationcenter.org/ findfunders/fundingsources/rfp.html. Specified deadlines are usually associated with strict timetables for agency or foundation review. Some programs have more than one application deadline during the fiscal or calendar year. Applicants should plan proposal development around the established deadlines.

Getting Organized to Write the Proposal

The grant seeker, having narrowed down the field of potential funders, may want to approach the most likely prospects to confirm that they might indeed be interested in the project. Many federal agencies and foundations are willing to provide an assessment of a preliminary one- or two-page concept paper before a formal proposal is prepared. The concept paper should give a brief description of the needs to be addressed, who is to carry out the project, what is to be accomplished, by what means, how long it will take, how the accomplishments will be measured, plans for the future, how much it will cost, and the ways this proposal relates to the mission of the funding source.

Developing a concept paper is excellent preparation for writing the final proposal. The grant seeker should try to see the project or activity from the viewpoint of the grant-making agency or foundation. Like the proposal, the concept paper should be brief, clear, and informative. It is important to understand that from the funder's vantage point, the grant is not seen as the end of the process, but only as the midpoint. The funder will want to know what will happen to the project once the grant ends. For example, will it be self-supporting or will it be used as a demonstration to apply for further funding? Will it need ongoing support, for how long, and what are the anticipated outcomes?

If the funding source expresses interest in the concept paper, the grant seeker can ask for suggestions, criticism, and guidance, before writing the final proposal.

Feedback and dialog are essential elements to a successful funding proposal.

Throughout the proposal writing stage, an applicant may want to keep a notebook or a file handy to write down or gather ideas and related materials for review. The gathering of documents such as articles of incorporation, tax exemption certificates, and bylaws should be completed, if possible, before the writing begins.

At the end of this chapter, useful websites cover proposal writing, give sample grant proposals (including a template for writing a proposal), and link to federal program information and grants management circulars.

WRITING AN EFFECTIVE GRANT PROPOSAL

Overall Considerations

An effective grant proposal has to make a compelling case. Not only must the idea be a good one, but so must the presentation. Things to be considered include the following:

- All of the requirements of the funding source must be met: prescribed format, necessary inclusions, deadlines, etc.
- The proposal should have a clear, descriptive title.
- The proposal should be a cohesive whole, building logically, with one section leading to another; this is an especially important consideration when several people have been involved in its preparation.
- Language should be clear and concise, devoid of jargon; explanations should be offered for acronyms and terms which may be unfamiliar to someone outside the field.
- Each of the parts of the proposal should provide as brief but informative a narrative as possible, with supporting data relegated to an appendix.

At various stages in the proposal writing process, the proposal should be reviewed by a number of interested and disinterested parties. Each time it has been critiqued, it may be necessary to rethink the project and its presentation. While such revision is necessary to clarify the proposal, one of the dangers is that the original excitement of those making the proposal sometimes gets written out. Somehow, this must be conveyed in the final proposal. Applicants are advised: make it interesting!

Basic Components of a Proposal

The basic sections of a standard grant proposal include the following:

1. Cover letter
2. Proposal summary or abstract
3. Introduction describing the grant seeker or organization

4. Problem statement (or needs assessment)
5. Project objectives
6. Project methods or design
7. Project evaluation
8. Future funding
9. Project budget

Cover Letter

The one-page cover letter should be written on the applicant's letterhead and should be signed by the organization's highest official. It should be addressed to the individual at the funding source with whom the organization has dealt, and should refer to earlier discussions. While giving a brief outline of the needs addressed in the proposal, the cover letter should demonstrate a familiarity with the mission of the grantmaking agency or foundation and emphasize the ways in which this project contributes to these goals.

Proposal Summary: Outline of Project Goals

The grant proposal summary outlines the proposed project and should appear at the beginning of the proposal. It could be in the form of a cover letter or a separate page, but should definitely be brief—no longer than two or three paragraphs.

The summary should be prepared after the grant proposal has been developed in order to encompass all the key points necessary to communicate the objectives of the project. It is this document that becomes the cornerstone of the proposal, and the initial impression it gives will be critical to the success of the venture. In many cases, the summary will be the first part of the proposal package seen by agency or foundation officials and very possibly could be the only part of the package that is carefully reviewed before the decision is made to consider the project any further. When letters of support are written, the summary may be used as justification for the project.

The summary should include a description of the applicant, a definition of the problem to be solved, a statement of the objectives to be achieved, an outline of the activities and procedures to be used to accomplish those objectives, a description of the evaluation design, plans for the project at the end of the grants, and a statement of what it will cost the funding agency. It may also identify other funding sources or entities participating in the project.

For federal funding, the applicant should develop a project which can be supported in view of the local need. Alternatives, in the absence of federal support, should be pointed out. The influence of the project both during and after the project period should be explained. The consequences of the project as a result of funding should be highlighted, for example, statistical projections of how many people might benefit from the project's accomplishments.

Introduction: Presenting a Credible Applicant

In the introduction, applicants describe their organization and demonstrate that they are qualified to carry out the proposed project—they establish their credibility and make the point that they are a good investment, in no more than a page. Statements made here should be carefully tailored, pointing out that the overall goals and purposes of the applicant are consistent with those of the funding source. This section should provide the following:

- A brief history of the organization, its past and present operations, its goals and mission, its significant accomplishments, any success stories.
- Reference should be made to grants, endorsements, and press coverage the organization has already received (with supporting documentation included in the appendix).
- Qualifications of its professional staff, and a list of its board of directors.
- Indicate whether funds for other parts of the project are being sought elsewhere; such evidence will strengthen the proposal, demonstrating to the reviewing officer that all avenues of support have been throughly explored.
- An individual applicant should include a succinct resume relating to the objectives of the proposal (what makes the applicant eligible to undertake the work or project?).

Problem Statement or Needs Assessment

This section lays out the reason for the proposal. It should make a clear, concise, and well- supported statement of the problem to be addressed, from the beneficiaries' viewpoint, in no more than two pages.

The best way to collect information about the problem is to conduct and document both a formal and informal needs assessment for a program in the target or service area. The information provided should be both factual and directly related to the problem addressed by the proposal. Areas to document are as follows:

- Purpose for developing the proposal.
- Beneficiaries—who are they and how will they benefit.
- Social and economic costs to be affected.
- Nature of the problem (provide as much hard evidence as possible).
- How the applicant or organization came to realize the problem exists, and what is currently being done about the problem.
- Stress what gaps exist in addressing the problem that will be addressed by the proposal.
- Remaining alternatives available when funding has been exhausted. Explain what will happen to the project and the impending implications.
- Most important, the specific manner through which problems might be solved. Review the resources needed, considering how they will be used and to what end.

One of the pitfalls to be avoided is defining the problem as a lack of program or facility (i.e., giving one of the possible solutions to a problem as the problem itself). For example, the lack of a medical center in an economically depressed area is not the problem—the problem is that poor people in the area have health needs that are not currently being addressed. The problem described should be of reasonable dimensions, with the targeted population and geographic area clearly defined. It should include a retrospective view of the situation, describing past efforts to ameliorate it, and making projections for the future. The problem statement, developed with input from the beneficiaries, must be supported by statistics and statements from authorities in the fields. The case must be made that the applicant, because of its history, demonstrable skills, and past accomplishments, is the right organization to solve the problem.

There is a considerable body of literature on the exact assessment techniques to be used. Any local, regional, or state government planning office, or local university offering course work in planning and evaluation techniques should be able to provide excellent background references. Types of data that may be collected include historical, geographic, quantitative, factual, statistical, and philosophical information, as well as studies completed by colleges, and literature searches from public or university libraries. Local colleges or universities which have a department or section related to the proposal topic may help determine if there is interest in developing a student or faculty project to conduct a needs assessment. It may be helpful to include examples of the findings for highlighting in the proposal.

Project Objectives: Goals and Desired Outcome

Once the needs have been described, proposed solutions have to be outlined, wherever possible in quantitative terms. The population to be served, time frame of the project, and specific anticipated outcomes must be defined. The figures used should be verifiable. If the proposal is funded, the stated objectives will probably be used to evaluate program progress, so they should be realistic. There is literature available to help identify and write program objectives.

It is important not to confuse objectives with methods or strategies toward those ends. For example, the objective should not be stated as "building a prenatal clinic in Adams County," but as "reducing the infant mortality rate in Adams County to X percent by a specific date." The concurrent strategy or method of accomplishing the stated objective may include the establishment of mobile clinics that bring services to the community.

Program Methods and Program Design: A Plan of Action

The program design refers to how the project is expected to work and solve the stated problem. Just as the statement of objectives builds upon the problem statement, the description of methods or strategies builds upon the statement of objectives. For each objective, a specific plan of action should be laid out. It should delineate a sequence of justifiable activities, indicating the proposed staffing and timetable for each task. This section should be carefully reviewed to make sure that what is being proposed is realistic in terms of the applicant's resources and time frame. Outline the following:

1. The activities to occur along with the related resources and staff needed to operate the project ("inputs").
2. A flow chart of the organizational features of the project: describe how the parts interrelate, where personnel will be needed, and what they are expected to do. Identify the kinds of facilities, transportation, and support services required ("throughputs").
3. Explain what will be achieved through 1 and 2 above ("outputs"), that is, plan for measurable results. Project staff may be required to produce evidence of program performance through an examination of stated objectives during either a site visit by the grantor agency or foundation, and/or grant reviews which may involve peer review committees.
4. It may be useful to devise a diagram of the program design. Such a procedure will help to conceptualize both the scope and detail of the project.

> **Example:**
>
> Draw a three-column block. Each column is headed by one of the parts (inputs, throughputs, and outputs), and on the left (next to the first column) specific program features should be identified (i.e., implementation, staffing, procurement, and systems development). In the grid, specify something about the program design, for example, assume the first column is labeled inputs and the first row is labeled staff. On the grid one might specify under inputs five nurses to operate a child care unit. The throughput might be to maintain charts, counsel the children, and set up a daily routine; outputs might be to discharge 25 healthy children per week.

5. Carefully consider the pressures of the proposed implementation, that is, the time and money needed to undertake each part of the plan. Wherever possible, justify in the narrative the course of action taken. The most economical method should be used that does not compromise or sacrifice project quality. The financial expenses associated with performance of the project will later become points of negotiation with the government or foundation program staff. If everything is not carefully justified in writing in the proposal, after

negotiation with the grantor agencies or foundations, the approved project may resemble less of the original concept.

> A Program Evaluation and Review Technique (PERT) chart could be useful and supportive in justifying some proposals. Larger projects can easily be laid out using commercial off-the-shelf project management software such as Microsoft Office Visio or Smart Draw. The software allows the project manager to construct a PERT chart that provides a graphical representation of all tasks in the project and the way tasks are related to each other. Such project manager software provides a variety of report formats that can be used to track project progress. The PERT chart and other related reports can be maintained on a network of computers so that all project participants can access the latest project information.

6. Highlight the innovative features of the proposal which could be considered distinct from other proposals under consideration.
7. Whenever possible, use appendixes to provide details, supplementary data, references, and information requiring in-depth analysis. These types of data, although supportive of the proposal, if included in the body of the proposal, could detract from its readability. Appendixes provide the proposal reader with immediate access to details if and when clarification of an idea, sequence or conclusion is required. Time tables, work plans, schedules, activities, methodologies, legal papers, personal vitae, letters of support, and endorsements are examples of appendixes.

Evaluation: Product and Process Analysis

An evaluation plan should be a consideration at every stage of the proposal's development. Data collected for the problem statement form a comparative basis for determining whether measurable objectives are indeed being met, and whether proposed methods are accomplishing these ends; or whether different parts of the plan need to be fine-tuned to be made more effective and efficient.

Among the considerations will be whether evaluation will be done by the organization itself or by outside experts. The organizations will have to decide whether outside experts have the standing in the field and the degree of objectivity that would justify the added expense, or whether the job could be done with sufficient expertise by its own staff, without taking too much time away from the project itself.

Methods of measurement, whether standardized tests, interviews, questionnaires, observation, etc., will depend upon the nature and scope of the project. Procedures and schedules for gathering, analyzing, and reporting data will need to be spelled out.

The evaluation component is two-fold: (1) product evaluation and (2) process evaluation. "Product evaluation" addresses results that can be attributed to the project, as well as the extent to which the project has satisfied its stated objectives. "Process evaluation" addresses how the project was conducted, in terms of consistency with the stated plan of action and the effectiveness of the various activities within the plan.

Most federal agencies now require some form of program evaluation among grantees. The requirements of the proposed project should be explored carefully. Evaluations may be conducted by an internal staff member, an evaluation firm or both. Many federal grants include a specific time frame for performance review and evaluation. For instance, several economic development programs require grant recipients to report on a quarterly and annual basis. In instances where there are no specified evaluation periods, the applicant should state the amount of time needed to evaluate, how the feedback will be disseminated among the proposed staff, and a schedule for review and comment. Evaluation designs may start at the beginning, middle, or end of a project, but the applicant should specify a start-up time. It is desirable and advisable to submit an evaluation design at the start of a project for two reasons:

- Convincing evaluations require the collection of appropriate baseline data before and during program operations; and
- If the evaluation design cannot be prepared at the outset then a critical review of the program design may be advisable.

Even if the evaluation design has to be revised as the project progresses, it is much easier and cheaper to modify a good design. If the problem is not well defined and carefully analyzed for cause and effect relationships, then a good evaluation design may be difficult to achieve. Sometimes a pilot study is needed to begin the identification of facts and relationships. Often a thorough literature search may be sufficient.

Evaluation requires both coordination and agreement among program decision makers. Above all, the federal grantor agency's or foundation's requirements should be highlighted in the evaluation design. Also, grantor agencies may require specific evaluation techniques such as designated data formats (an existing information collection system) or they may offer financial inducements for voluntary participation in a national evaluation study. The applicant should ask specifically about these points. Also, for federal programs, consult the "Criteria For Selecting Proposals" section of the CFDA program description to determine the exact evaluation methods to be required for a specific program if funded.

Future Funding

The last narrative part of the proposal explains what will happen to the program once the grant ends. It should describe a plan for continuation beyond the grant period, and outline all other contemplated fund-raising efforts and future plans for applying for additional grants. Projections for operating and maintaining facilities and equipment should also be given. The applicant may discuss maintenance and future program funding if program funds are for construction activity; and may account for other needed expenditures if program includes purchase of equipment.

Budget Development and Requirements

Although the degree of specificity of any budget will vary depending upon the nature of the project and the requirements of the funding source, a complete, well-thought-out budget serves to reinforce the applicant's credibility and to increase the likelihood of the proposal being funded. The estimated expenses in the budget should build upon the justifications given in the narrative section of the proposal. A well-prepared budget should be reasonable and demonstrate that the funds being asked for will be used wisely. The budget should be as concrete and specific as possible in its estimates. Every effort should be made to be realistic, to estimate costs accurately, and not to underestimate staff time.

The budget format should be as clear as possible. It should begin with a Budget Summary, which, like the Proposal Summary, is written after the entire budget has been prepared. Each section of the budget should be in outline form, listing line items under major headings and subdivisions. Each of the major components should be subtotaled with a grand total placed at the end. If the funding source provides forms, most of these elements can simply be filled into the appropriate spaces.

Generally, budgets are divided into two categories, personnel costs and non-personnel costs. In preparing the budget, the applicant may first review the proposal and make lists of items needed for the project. The personnel section usually includes a breakdown of the following items:

- salaries (including increases in multiyear projects),
- fringe benefits such as health insurance and retirement plans, and
- consultant and contract services.

The items in the non-personnel section will vary widely, but may include

- space/office rental or leasing costs,
- utilities,
- purchase or rental of equipment,
- training to use new equipment, and
- photocopying, office supplies.

Some hard to pin down budget areas are: utilities, rental of buildings and equipment, salary increases, food, telephones, insurance, and transportation. Budget adjustments are sometimes made after the grant award, but this can be a lengthy process. The applicant should be certain that implementation, continuation, and phase-down costs can be met. Costs associated with leases, evaluation systems, hard/soft match requirements, audits, development, implementation and maintenance of information and accounting systems, and other long-term financial commitments should be considered.

A well-prepared budget justifies all expenses and is consistent with the proposal narrative. Some areas in need of an evaluation for consistency are as follows:

- Salaries in the proposal in relation to those of the applicant organization should be similar.
- If new staff persons are being hired, additional space and equipment should be considered, as necessary.

- If the budget calls for an equipment purchase, it should be the type allowed by the grantor agency.
- If additional space is rented, the increase in insurance should be supported.
- In the case of federal grants, if an indirect cost rate applies to the proposal, such as outlined by the Office of Management and Budget (OMB) in Circulars such as numbers A-122, A-21, and A-87 (see http://www.whitehouse.gov/omb/grants/grants_circulars.html), the division between direct and indirect costs should not be in conflict, and the aggregate budget totals should refer directly to the approved formula.
- If matching funds are required, the contributions to the matching fund should be taken out of the budget unless otherwise specified in the application instructions.

In learning to develop a convincing budget and determining appropriate format, reviewing other grant proposals is often helpful. The applicant may ask government agencies and foundations for copies of winning grants proposals. Grants seekers may find the following examples of grants budgets helpful:

- Budget Information, Instructions and Forms
  http://www.neh.gov/grants
- Foundation Center: Examples of Nonprofit Budgets
  http://foundationcenter.org/getstarted/faqs/html/samplebudget.html
- Getting Your Grant Proposal Budget Right
  http://nonprofit.about.com/od/foundationfundinggrants/a/grantbudget.htm
- Grant-writing Tools for Non-Profit Organizations: Full Proposal Budget http://www.npguides.org/guide/budget.htm
- Proposal Budgeting Basics
  http://foundationcenter.org/getstarted/tutorials/prop_budgt/index.html
- UWRF Grants Office: Budgets (University of Wisconsin) http://www.uwrf.edu/grants

In preparing budgets for government grants, the applicant may keep in mind that funding levels of federal assistance programs change yearly. It is useful to review the appropriations and average grants or loans awarded over the past several years to try to project future funding levels: see "Financial

Information" section of the CFDA program description for fiscal year appropriations and estimates; and "Range and Average of Financial Assistance" for prior years' awards. However, it is safer never to anticipate that the income from the grant will be the sole support for larger projects. This consideration should be given to the overall budget requirements, and in particular, to budget line items most subject to inflationary pressures. Restraint is important in determining inflationary cost projections (avoid padding budget line items), but the applicant may attempt to anticipate possible future increases.

For federal grants, it is also important to become familiar with grants management requirements. The CFDA identifies in the program description OMB circulars applicable to each federal program. Applicants should review appropriate documents while developing a proposal budget because they are essential in determining items such as cost principles, administrative and audit requirements and compliance, and conforming with government guidelines for federal domestic assistance. OMB circulars are available in full text on the Web at http://www.whitehouse.gov/ omb/grants/grants_circulars.html.

To coordinate federal grants to states, Executive Order 12372, "Intergovernmental Review of Federal Programs," was issued to foster intergovernmental partnership and strengthen federalism by relying on state and local processes for the coordination and review of proposed Federal financial assistance and direct federal development. The executive order allows each state to designate an office to perform this function, addresses of which may be found at the OMB website at *http://www.whitehouse. gov/omb/grants/spoc.html*. States that are not listed on this Web page have chosen not to participate in the intergovernmental review process. If the applicant is located within one of these states, he or she may still send application materials directly to a federal awarding agency. State and regional offices of federal agencies that award grants and other domestic assistance can be found in CFDA Appendix IV at http://12.46.245.173/CFDA/pdf/appx4.pdf.

Proposal Appendix

Lengthy documents that are referred to in the narrative are best added to the proposal in an appendix. Examples include letters of endorsement, partial list of previous funders, key staff resumes, annual reports, statistical data, maps, pictorial material, and newspaper and magazine articles about the organizations. Nonprofit organizations should include an IRS 501(c)(3) Letter of Tax Exempt Status.

ADDITIONAL PROPOSAL WRITING WEBSITES

All About Grants Tutorials (National Institutes of Health)
http://www.niaid.nih.gov/ncn/grants
Grant Writing Tips Sheet http://grants1.nih.gov/grants

EPA Purdue University Grant-Writing Tutorial (Environmental Protection Agency)
http://www.purdue.edu/envirosoft/grants

Grant-writing Tools for Non-Profit Organizations (Non-Profit Guides)
http://www.npguides.org/
Sample proposals: http://www.npguides.org/guide/sample

Proposal Writing Short Course (Foundation Center; English and Spanish)
http://fdncenter.org/learn/shortcourse/prop1.html
Where can I find examples of grant proposals?
http://foundationcenter.org/getstarted/faqs/html/propsample.html

Sample Proposals (SchoolGrants.org)
http://www.k12grants.org/samples/

Selected Proposal Writing Websites (University of Pittsburgh)
http://www.pitt.edu/~offres/proposal/propwriting/websites

Tips on Writing a Grant Proposal (Environmental Protection Agency)
http://www.epa.gov/ogd/recipient/tips.htm

What Reviewers Look For (College of William and Mary)
http://www.wm.edu/grants

Writing a Successful Grant Proposal (Minnesota Council on Foundations)
http://www.mcf.org/mcf/grant/writing

In: A Government Guide to Grants
Editors: Nathan E. Legaspi

ISBN: 978-1-60876-751-9
© 2010 Nova Science Publishers, Inc.

Chapter 4

RESOURCES FOR GRANT SEEKERS

Merete F. Gerli

SUMMARY

This chapter describes key sources of information on government and private funding, and outlines eligibility for federal grants. Federal grants are intended for projects benefiting states and communities. Individuals may be eligible for other kinds of benefits or assistance, or small businesses and students may be eligible for loans. Free information is readily available to grantseekers who generally know best the details of their projects. The Catalog of Federal Domestic Assistance (CFDA) describes 1600 federal programs, 1000 of them grants, and can be searched by keyword, subject, department or agency, program title, beneficiary, and applicant eligibility. Federal department and agency web sites provide additional information and guidance, and provide state agency contacts. Once a program has been identified, eligible grantseekers may apply electronically for grants at the website Grants.gov through a uniform process for all agencies. Through Grants.gov, they may identify when federal funding notices and deadlines for a CFDA program become available, sign up for e-mail notification of funding opportunities, and track the progress of submitted applications.

Since government funds may be limited, the report also discusses sources of private and corporate foundation funding. The Foundation Center is a clearinghouse for information about private, corporate, and community foundations, with collections of resources in every state.

Included in this chapter are sources of information on writing grant proposals. See also CRS Report RL32 159, *How to Develop and Write a Grant Proposal*, by Merete F. Gerli.

Sources described in this chapter are also included in the CRS website WG02001, Grants and Federal Domestic Assistance Web Page, by Merete F. Gerli. Upon request, this website may be added to a Member's home page. For congressional staff, see also CRS Report RL34035, *Grants Work in a Congressional Office*, by Merete F. Gerli.

INTRODUCTION

Congressional offices are often approached by constituents seeking grants for projects, including local governments, nonprofit groups, community organizations, small businesses, and individuals. Though many hope for federal funding, such assistance is often limited and other funding sources such as private foundations should be considered.

Federal grants are not benefits or entitlements to individuals. Grants are intended for projects serving state, community, and local needs. Most federal funding goes to state and local governments, which in turn may make sub-awards to local entities such as eligible nonprofit organizations. Local governments seeking funds for community services, infrastructure, and economic revitalization may be eligible to tap into state or federal funds. Government assistance may also be available for nonprofit organizations, including faith-based groups, for initiatives such as establishing soup kitchens or after-school tutoring programs benefitting entire communities.

For others, such as for individuals seeking financial help, starting or expanding a small business, or needing funds for education, benefits or loans may be available.

- Individuals looking for government benefits (such as for child or health care, housing or energy costs, disability or veterans needs, or "living assistance") may find useful the website GovBenefits.gov at http://www.govbenefits.gov.
- Students seeking financial aid can search Student Aid on the Web at http://www.Studentaid.ed.gov.

- To start or expand a small business, the federal government provides help in the form of loans, advisory, and technical assistance. See the Small Business Administration (SBA) website at http://www.sba.gov to find programs and state or local SBA offices.

Groups seeking funding for projects need first to determine the most appropriate sources of funds. Because government funds may be limited, sources of private funding should also be considered. State and community foundations may be particularly interested in funding local projects; many projects may require a combination of government and private funding. Local business or foundation funding might be appropriate for supporting local memorials or programs. Community fund-raising may be more suitable for school enrichment activities such as band or sports uniforms or field trips.

For eligible state and local governments and nonprofit organizations, identifying appropriate programs, and then contacting federal and state agencies early in the process, before submitting formal applications, is recommended. State-located federal offices often handle federal grant applications and disbursement of funds. State government departments and agencies also fund projects and administer federal block grants.

WHO IS ELIGIBLE FOR A GOVERNMENT GRANT?

There are many groups or organizations that are eligible to apply for government grants. Typically, most grantee entities fall into the following categories:[1]

- Government Organizations
    - State Governments
    - Local Governments
    - City or Township Governments
    - Special District Governments
    - Native American Tribal Governments (federally recognized)
    - Native American Tribal Governments (other than federally recognized)
- Education Organizations
    - Independent School Districts
    - Public and State Controlled Institutions of Higher Education

- Private Institutions of Higher Education
- Public Housing Organizations
  - Public Housing Authorities
  - Indian Housing Authorities
- Non-Profit Organizations
  - Nonprofits having a 501(c)(3) status with the IRS, other than institutions of higher education
  - Nonprofits that do not have a 501(c)(3) status with the IRS, other than institutions of higher education
- For-Profit Organizations (other than small businesses)

Some constituents may have seen or heard media advertisements claiming federal grants are available to help them. However, the Federal Trade Commission (FTC), the nation's consumer protection agency, cautions grantseekers:[2]

> Sometimes, it's an ad that claims you will qualify to receive a "free grant" to pay for education costs, home repairs, home business expenses, or unpaid bills. Other times, it's a phone call supposedly from a "government" agency or some other organization with an official sounding name. In either case, the claim is the same: your application for a grant is guaranteed to be accepted, and you'll never have to pay the money back.

But, warns the FTC, these "money for nothing" grant offers usually are misleading, whether you see them in your local paper or a national magazine, or hear about them on the phone. Consumers should beware of paying "processing fees" for information that is available free to the public. Ads claiming federal grants are available for home repairs, home business, unpaid bills, or other personal expenses are often a scam.

KEY FEDERAL SOURCES

Catalog of Federal Domestic Assistance (General Services Administration) http://www.cfda.gov

The Catalog of Federal Domestic Assistance (CFDA) is the primary source of information on federal grants and nonfinancial assistance programs. Actual funding depends upon annual budget appropriations. For example some authorized federal programs may be described in the Catalog but Congress may choose not to fund them in a certain budget year. Once a program is identified in CFDA, for current notices of funding availability and to apply, see Grants.gov (below). Key features of CFDA include the following.

- Describes some 1,600 federal domestic assistance programs, financial and nonfinancial assistance programs administered by the departments and agencies of the federal government; approximately 1000 of these are grants programs.
- Allows grantseekers to identify federal programs that might provide support for their projects, either directly, or through grants to states and local governments that in turn make sub-awards to local grantseekers.
- Available free to the public, searchable full-text, and updated continuously on the Web.
- Enables searching by keyword; or by other useful browsable listings, such as by subject, by department or agency, by applicant eligibility, by beneficiary, or by other category.
- For each program, describes objectives of the program, eligibility requirements, the application and award process, post assistance requirements, past fiscal year obligations and future estimates, program accomplishments and examples of funded projects, related CFDA programs, and information contacts, including regional or local offices of federal agencies if applicable.
- Links to department and agency websites and to Office of Management and Budget (OMB) circulars affecting program management and record-keeping requirements.
- Includes information on developing and writing grant proposals: provides guidance in formulating federal grant applications, proposal development, basic components of a proposal, review recommendations, and referral to federal guidelines and literature.

Although more easily searchable and continuously updated on the Internet, the printed *Catalog* is available to the public in local government depository libraries in every state; see addresses of libraries at http://www.gpoaccess.gov/libraries.html.

Grants.gov (via U.S. Department of Health and Human Services) http://www.grants

After grantseekers identify federal programs in CFDA and contact agencies (see section below), they may be directed to the website Grants.gov to apply for federal grants when application announcements for competitive grants become available. The website allows grantseekers to register and download applications for current competitive funding opportunities from all 26 federal grants-making agencies. Grantseekers themselves can check on notices of funding availability (NOFAs) or requests for proposals (RFPs); sign up to receive e-mail notification of grant opportunities; and apply for federal grants online through a unified process. The site also guides grantseekers in obtaining Dun and Bradstreet (DUNS) numbers, required for all federal grants.

To download and submit an application from Grants.gov, registration is required. The site provides a narrated tutorial on how to complete a grant application package and a Frequently Asked Questions (FAQs) page. Once an application is submitted, grants applicants themselves can then track progress of their application using their unique ID and password. Applications can be identified by CFDA number, funding opportunity number, competition ID, and/or Grants.gov tracking number.

FEDERAL CONTACTS IN STATES AND STATE ADMINISTERING AGENCIES (SAAs)

For eligible state and local governments and nonprofit organizations, after identifying appropriate programs it is recommended grantseekers contact federal and state agencies early in the process, before submitting formal applications. State-located federal offices often handle federal grant applications and disbursement of funds. State government departments and agencies also fund projects and administer federal block grants.

Federal Agency Regional and Local Office Addresses (from CFDA) http://www.cfda.gov/CFDA/pdf/appx4.pdf

Many federal department and agencies have state or regional offices that grantseekers can contact for additional program information and application procedures. For listings, consult CFDA Appendix IV, Federal Agency Regional and Local Office Addresses. Much of the federal grant budget moves to the states through formula and block grants. State, regional, and local federal offices often handle grants applications and funds disbursement. Each federal agency has its own procedures: applicants should call the department

Resources for Grant Seekers

or agency in question before applying for funding to obtain the most up-to-date information.

State Administering Agencies

Many federal grants such as formula and block grants are awarded directly to state governments, which then set priorities and allocate funds within that state. For more information on how a state intends to distribute federal formula funds, grantseekers can contact the State Administering Agency (SAA). State government agencies are familiar with federal program requirements, can assist local governments and nonprofit organizations with proposals, and can provide other guidance.

Many federal department and agency websites include SAAs and often the site will have an interactive U.S. map. Grantseekers can click on their state and obtain program and state contact information. A selection of some executive department websites includes the following:[3]

- Agriculture Rural Development State Contacts
  http://www.rurdev.usda.gov/recd_map.html
- National Endowment for the Arts (NEA) Partners
  http://www.arts.gov/partner/state/SAA_RAO_list.html
- Commerce Offices and Services
  http://www.commerce
- Education (ED) State Contacts
  http://www.ed.gov/about/contacts/state/index.html
- Energy (DOE) State Contacts
  http://www.eere.energy
- Environmental Protection Agency (EPA) Grant Regional Office
  http://www.epa.gov/ogd/grants
- Federal Emergency Management Agency (FEMA) State Offices and Agencies http://www.fema.gov/about/contact/statedr.shtm
- Health and Human Services (HHS), Administration on Children and Families: State Contacts
  http://www.acf.hhs.gov/acf_contact_us.html#state
- Homeland Security (DHS) State Contacts and Grant Award Information http://www.dhs.gov/xgovt/grants
- Housing and Urban Development (HUD) State/Local Offices
  http://www.hud.gov/localoffices.cfm
- National Endowment for the Humanities (NEA) State Councils
  http://www.neh.gov/whoweare/statecouncils.html

- Office of Justice Programs (OJP) State Administering Agencies http://www.ojp.usdoj.gov/saa/
- Labor (DOL) Education and Training Administration, State Contacts http://www.doleta.gov/regions/statecontacts/
- Small Business Administration http://www.sba.gov/localresources/index.html
- Transportation, Federal Transit Administration (FTA) Regional Offices http://www.fta.dot.gov/regional
- Veterans Affairs State/Territory Offices http://www.va.gov/statedva.htm

State Single Point of Contact (Office of Management and Budget) http://www.whitehouse.gov/omb/grants

States often require federal grants applicants to submit a copy of their application for state government review and comment, and many (but not all) have designated a state Single Point of Contact (SPOC). The state offices listed here coordinate government grants development and may provide guidance to grantseekers.

RELATED FEDERAL SOURCES

A-Z Index of U.S. Government Departments and Agencies (General Services Administration)
http://www.usa.gov/Agencies/Federal/All_Agencies/index.shtml

To better develop a grant proposal, search a department or agency's home page to learn more about its programs and objectives. The site also includes the following:

- Government Benefits, Grants and Financial Aid http://www.usa.gov/Citizen/Topics/Benefits.shtml
- Grants and Financial Management http://www.usa.gov/Government/State_Local/Grants.shtml
  Covers grants management, federal assistance programs, resources about acquisition and procurement, financial management, and taxes.
- Grants, Loans, and Other Assistance http://www.usa.gov/Business/Nonprofit.shtml

Links to federal department and agency information and services, fundraising and outreach, grants, loans and other assistance, laws and regulations, management and operations, registration and licensing, and taxes.
- Businesses and Nonprofits
  http://www.usa.gov/Business/Business_Gateway.shtml
  Links to useful sites, including financial assistance, for small business, government contractors, and foreign business in the United States.

Faith-Based and Community Initiatives (FBCI, Office of the President) http://www.whitehouse.gov/government

The FBCI initiative identified federal programs for which faith-based and community organizations may apply. The following FBCI publications may be of help to organizations seeking funds.

- Guidance to Faith-Based and Community Organizations on Partnering with the Federal Government *http://www.whitehouse.gov/government*
- Federal Funds for Organizations That Help Those in Need *http://www.whitehouse.gov/government* Describes some 170 federal programs, many of which can be applied for directly. Some are "formula grants" made available to states and local governments, which in turn award funds to grassroots and local organizations. For those, grantseekers must contact local and state agencies responsible for managing the programs.
- A Guide to Federal Economic Development Programs for Faith-Based and Community Organizations http://www.whitehouse.gov/government Presents a categorized listing of sample economic development efforts funded by the federal government, for service organizations interested in strengthening economic projects of individuals, communities, and businesses.

Homeland Security State Contacts & Grants Award Information (U.S. Department of Homeland Security)
  http://www.dhs.gov/xgovt/grants

Click on map for state allocations and contact information. Most Homeland Security non-disaster grant programs are designated for state and local governments and specific entities such as colleges, etc. Unsolicited applications from individuals are generally not accepted. Includes Urban Area

Security Initiative, Citizens Corps, Medical Response System, Operation Stonegarden (border security), and Infrastructure Protection. Assistance to Firefighters may be found at http://www.firegrantsupport.com/.

Grants Management Website (Office of Management and Budget)
http://www.whitehouse.gov/omb/grants

OMB establishes government-wide grants management policies and guidelines through circulars and common rules. OMB Circulars are cited in CFDA program descriptions.

PRIVATE, CORPORATE, AND ADDITIONAL FUNDING SOURCES

Foundation Center
http://www.foundationcenter.org/

Information gateway to the grant seeking process, private funding sources (including national, state, community, and corporate foundations), guidelines on writing a grants proposal, addresses of libraries in every state with grants reference collections, and links to other useful Internet websites. The Center maintains a comprehensive database on foundation grantsmanship, publishes directories and guides, conducts research and publishes studies in the field, and offers a variety of training and educational seminars. Free information on the website includes the following:

- Guide to Funding Research
  http://foundationcenter.org/getstarted/tutorials/gfr/index.html
- Foundation Finder
  http://lnp.foundationcenter.org/finder.html
  Search for information about more than 70,000 private and community foundations.
- Proposal Writing Short Course
  http://fdncenter.org/learn/shortcourse/prop1.html
  Free tutorial on developing a good grant proposal; also in Spanish, French, and other languages.

- Foundation Center Cooperating Collections
  http://foundationcenter.org/collections/

Libraries in every state providing the Foundation Directory Online and free funding information for grantseekers.

Community Foundations Locator (Council on Foundations)
http://www.cof.org/Locator/index.cfm?crumb=2
Community foundations are often particularly interested in local projects and maintain diverse grants programs.

Funding Sources (Grantsmanship Center)
http://tgci.com/funding
The website provides listings by state of top grantmaking, community, and corporate foundations that grantseekers might consider in identifying likely sources of private foundation funding.

Grants and Related Resources (Michigan State University Libraries)
http://www.lib.msu.edu/harris23/grants
Government and private grants resources, primarily Web, by subject or group categories, updated frequently. Includes listings for nonprofits, individuals, and businesses.

- Grants for Nonprofits
  http://www.lib.msu.edu/harris23/grants
- Grants for Individuals
  http://www.lib.msu.edu/harris23/grants
- Funding for Business and Economic Development
  http://www.lib.msu.edu/harris23/grants

GRANT PROPOSAL WRITING WEBSITES

A number of websites provide guidance, tips, and sample proposals. Constituents may also request from congressional offices CRS Report RL32159, *How to Develop and Write a Grant Proposal*, by Merete F. Gerli, which discusses standard content and formats. Websites that may be useful include the following:

- Developing and Writing Grant Proposals (CFDA) http://12.46.245.173/pls/portal30/CATALOG.GRANT_PROPOSAL_DYN.show
- Grant-Writing Tutorial (Environmental Protection Agency and Purdue University) http://www.purdue.edu/envirosoft/grants
- Grant-writing Tools for Non-Profit Organizations http://www.npguides.org/ (includes sample proposals at http://www.npguides.org/ guide/sample_proposals.htm)
- Proposal Writing Short Course (Foundation Center) http://fdncenter.org/learn/shortcourse/prop1.html (also has sample proposals)
- Sample Proposals (SchoolGrants.org) http://www.k12grants.org/samples/
- Selected Proposal Writing Websites (University of Pittsburgh) http://www.pitt.edu/~offres/proposal/propwriting/websites
- What Reviewers Look For (College of William and Mary) http://www.wm.edu/grants
- Writing a Successful Grant Proposal (Minnesota Council on Foundations) http://www.mcf.org/mcf/grant/writing

End Notes

[1] Grants.gov website Who is Eligible for a Grant? at http://www.grants

[2] Federal Trade Commission, FTC Consumer Alert, "Free Government Grants: Don't Take Them For Grant-ed," September 2006; at http://www.ftc.gov/bcp/edu/pubs/consumer/alerts/alt134.shtm.

[3] Compiled by CRS from executive department and agency websites.

CHAPTER SOURCES

The following chapters have been previously published:

Chapter 1 – This is an edited, excerpted and augmented edition of a United States Congressional Research Service publication, Report Order Code R40486, dated April 3, 2009.

- Chapter 2 – This is an edited, excerpted and augmented edition of a United States Congressional Research Service publication, Report Order Code RL34035, dated June 15, 2009.

Chapter 3 – This is an edited, excerpted and augmented edition of a United States Congressional Research Service publication, Report Order Code RL32159, dated June 9, 2009.

Chapter 4 - This is an edited, excerpted and augmented edition of a United States Congressional Research Service publication, Report Order Code RL34012, dated January 7, 2009.

INDEX

A

accountability, viii, 1, 3, 9, 14, 20
accounting, 4, 5, 19, 77
achievement, viii, 2, 3
administration, 4, 6, 13, 16
administrative, vii, x, 4, 6, 8, 10, 11, 16, 18, 39, 48, 61, 79
administrators, 4, 9, 11, 32
advertisements, 84
advocacy, ix, 27, 32
affiliates, 42
after-school, 29, 82
age, 16
aggressive behavior, 42
aid, vii, viii, ix, 1, 2, 3, 8, 12, 16, 19, 28, 29, 31, 35, 59, 82
aiding, 21, 39
alcohol, 42
alcohol use, 42
alternatives, x, 28, 55, 71
amendments, 18
American Recovery and Reinvestment Act, vii, 1, 2, 21, 25, 51
analysts, 13
appendix, 40, 52, 54, 68, 70, 79
application, 4, 31, 34, 35, 36, 38, 40, 42, 43, 44, 49, 50, 51, 53, 54, 62, 66, 78, 79, 84, 85, 86, 88
appropriations, ix, 7, 28, 32, 36, 38, 45, 46, 53, 78, 84
appropriations bills, 46
Appropriations Committee, 46
argument, 11
assessment, 15, 35, 67, 69, 71, 72
assessment techniques, 72
assets, 14, 23, 55
attacks, 21
auditing, 17
authority, viii, 1, 3, 15, 16
availability, 50, 85, 86
awareness, 17

B

benefits, x, 12, 29, 35, 49, 77, 81, 82
block grants, vii, viii, ix, 1, 2, 3, 4, 5, 6, 7, 8, 9, 10, 11, 12, 13, 14, 15, 16, 17, 18, 19, 20, 28, 36, 43, 45, 47, 53, 65, 83, 86, 87
blurring, 6
bonus, 16
border security, 90
breakdown, 77
budget deficit, 19
budget line, 79
buildings, 44, 48, 55, 64, 77
bureaucracy, 8
Bush Administration, 14, 23

C

caps, 49
cast, 65
Catalog of Federal Domestic Assistance, ix, x, 12, 28, 38, 44, 46, 49, 57, 58, 61, 65, 81, 84
catalyst, 53
categorical grants, viii, 2, 3, 4, 5, 6, 9, 10, 12, 13, 15, 17, 18, 19, 20, 21, 22, 47
category a, 8
CCR, 51, 66
Census Bureau, 4
child abuse, 21
Child Care Development Block Grant, viii, 1, 3
children, 16, 42, 73
citizens, 48, 58
civilian, 49
clinics, 72
colleges, 72, 89
commerce, 54, 87
commodities, 48
common rule, 58, 90
communities, x, 11, 16, 21, 29, 33, 35, 42, 43, 48, 81, 82, 89
community, vii, x, xi, 1, 2, 15, 17, 18, 21, 28, 29, 35, 39, 41, 45, 55, 56, 57, 61, 63, 64, 65, 72, 82, 83, 89, 90, 91
Community Development Block Grant (CDBG), viii, 1, 3, 7, 11, 12, 16, 17, 18, 22, 23, 24
community service, 29, 82
Community Services Block Grant, 7, 24
community support, vii, x, 39, 45, 61, 63, 64
compensation, 21
competition, 30, 36, 47, 56, 86
competitive process, 41
complement, 53
compliance, 79
components, 77, 85
computer software, 32, 39
confidence, 42
conflict, 78

Congress, 6, 8, 9, 11, 12, 13, 16, 17, 18, 19, 23, 24, 25, 27, 28, 43, 45, 46, 52, 57, 64, 84
congressional budget, 45
consolidation, 12, 24
constituent service, 30
constraints, 6, 56
construction, 29, 44, 47, 76
consulting, 62
consumer protection, 84
continuity, 32, 33
contractors, 58, 89
contracts, 33, 63
control, viii, 2, 3, 4, 15, 44
conversion, 18
COPS, 33
corporations, 39, 56, 64
cost saving, 10
cost-effective, 10
costs, 10, 11, 19, 71, 76, 77, 78, 82, 84
counsel, 48, 73
counseling, 53
course work, 72
covering, 37, 51, 63
credentials, 35, 40
credibility, 35, 70, 76
credit, 9, 14
crime, 21, 42
criminal justice, 42
criminal justice system, 42
criticism, 67
curriculum development, 33

D

data collection, 11
database, 43, 90
de novo, 17, 18
decentralization, viii, 1, 3
decision makers, 76
decisions, viii, 2, 3, 14, 35, 36, 45, 46
defaults, 47
deficiency, 11
democracy, 8
demographic change, 10

Index

Department of Agriculture, 7, 16, 38
Department of Commerce, 16
Department of Education, 7, 29
Department of Energy, 7, 25
Department of Health and Human Services, 7, 16, 21, 51, 85
Department of Homeland Security, 7, 21, 25, 89
Department of Housing and Urban Development, 7, 16, 38
Department of Justice, 7, 20, 21, 25
Department of Transportation, 7
depressed, 71
detention, 20
devolution, viii, 1, 3, 15, 19
disability, 82
disappointment, 41, 43
disaster, 89
disbursement, 83, 86
discipline, 11
discretionary, 18, 29, 45, 46, 47, 51
distress, 30
distribution, 11, 48
domestic issues, viii, 2, 3, 12
download, 51, 66, 86
drug treatment, 21
drugs, 48
duplication, 10, 15, 31, 63
duties, 37

E

economic development, 15, 18, 38, 75, 89
Economic Development Administration, 16
education, 7, 8, 18, 29, 33, 42, 54, 55, 83, 84, 87, 88
elderly, 11
eligibility criteria, 4
endorsements, 70, 74
energy, 18, 21, 25, 54, 82, 87
energy efficiency, 21
Energy Efficiency and Conservation Block Grant, vii, 1, 3, 7, 8, 21, 25
Energy Independence and Security Act, 21
enrollment, 10

entitlement programs, 10, 15, 16, 45
Environmental Protection Agency (EPA), 54, 80, 87, 92
Executive Branch, 9, 17, 23
Executive Order, 54, 79
exercise, 31
expenditures, 15, 16, 45, 76
expertise, 55, 75

F

failure, 15
faith, 29, 62, 82, 89
family, 56, 65
FDA, 50
federal budget, 11, 16, 66
Federal Emergency Management Agency, (FEMA),21, 54, 87
Federal Funding Accountability and Transparency Act, 43
federal funds, ix, 12, 27, 29, 30, 34, 36, 43, 44, 45, 47, 53, 82
federal government, vii, 1, 2, 13, 15, 19, 21, 22, 29, 47, 48, 50, 51, 54, 58, 65, 83, 85, 89
federal grants, vii, ix, x, 6, 12, 19, 20, 21, 27, 28, 29, 37, 38, 41, 50, 53, 54, 55, 65, 66, 75, 78, 79, 81, 84, 86, 87, 88
Federal Register, 50
Federal Trade Commission (FTC), 29, 84, 92
Federal Transit Administration (FTA), 55, 88
federalism, vii, viii, 2, 3, 6, 8, 9, 10, 11, 13, 19, 79
feedback, 75
fees, 13, 84
financial aid, 29, 59, 82
financial support, 16
fire, x, 28
flexibility, 5, 6, 10, 11, 12, 14, 15, 16, 20
focusing, 15, 16
food, 7, 19, 48, 77
food stamps, 7, 19
foreign language, 39

formula, viii, 2, 3, 4, 8, 9, 11, 14, 17, 22, 29, 36, 41, 45, 49, 50, 51, 53, 65, 78, 86, 87, 89
formula-project, viii, 2, 3
fossil fuel, 21
Foundation Center, x, xi, 39, 56, 57, 61, 65, 66, 78, 80, 81, 90, 92
foundations, x, xi, 28, 30, 31, 33, 39, 53, 55, 56, 57, 61, 62, 63, 64, 65, 66, 67, 74, 78, 82, 83, 90, 91
fragmentation, 14, 17
freedom, 16
fringe benefits, 77
fuel, 21
fundraising, 58, 89
funds, ix, xi, 4, 6, 7, 8, 10, 11, 12, 16, 17, 21, 22, 27, 29, 31, 40, 41, 43, 44, 46, 47, 53, 55, 56, 65, 66, 70, 76, 78, 81, 82, 83, 86, 87, 89

G

gene, 6
General Accounting Office, 22, 24, 25
General Services Administration (GSA), 49, 58, 84, 88
generalizations, 6
goals, vii, viii, x, 2, 3, 14, 15, 35, 37, 39, 49, 56, 61, 63, 69, 70
government, vii, viii, ix, x, xi, 1, 2, 3, 4, 5, 6, 7, 8, 9, 10, 11, 12, 13, 14, 15, 16, 19, 21, 22, 27, 28, 29, 34, 35, 36, 37, 41, 44, 45, 47, 48, 49, 50, 51, 52, 53, 54, 58, 59, 61, 62, 63, 64, 65, 66, 72, 73, 78, 79, 81, 82, 83, 84, 85, 86, 87, 88, 89, 90
Government Accountability Office (GAO), 4, 6, 23
government spending, viii, 2, 3, 12
governors, 19
GPO, 5, 22, 23, 24, 25
grants coordinator, ix, 27, 30
grants specialist, ix, x, 27, 28, 30, 35, 55
grassroots, 8, 9, 89
groups, x, 9, 12, 16, 17, 28, 29, 37, 42, 63, 64, 66, 82, 83

guidance, x, 37, 39, 41, 53, 54, 57, 67, 81, 85, 87, 88, 91
guidelines, x, 49, 50, 56, 58, 61, 62, 79, 85, 90

H

health, 13, 17, 18, 22, 30, 71, 77, 82
Health and Human Services (HHS), 7, 16, 18, 21, 42, 51, 55, 85, 87
health care, 17, 22, 82
health insurance, 77
higher education, 84
historical overview, vii, viii, 2, 3
homeland security, x, 21, 28, 41, 44, 65
Homeland Security, 7, 21, 25, 55, 87, 89
House Appropriations Committee, 46
housing, 14, 82
Housing and Urban Development (HUD), 7, 16, 38, 55, 87

I

identification, 40, 75
implementation, 6, 51, 73, 77
incentives, 11
income, 11, 12, 18, 79
Indian, 7, 17, 21, 84
infant mortality rate, 72
inflation, 12
inflationary pressures, 79
infrastructure, 29, 44, 82
institutions, 47, 55, 64, 66, 84
institutions of higher education, 84
instructional activities, 48
insurance, 77, 78
intentions, 64
interest groups, 17
Internal Revenue Service (IRS), 55, 57, 65, 80, 84
investment, 70

Index

J

job training, 12, 19
judges, 20
jurisdiction, 13, 19
jurisdictions, 11, 41, 44
justice, 13, 42
Justice Assistance Grant, viii, 1, 3, 7, 21, 25
Justice Department, 33
justification, 69
juveniles, 21

L

law, vii, 1, 2, 17, 18, 21, 43
law enforcement, vii, 1, 2, 17, 21
laws, 58, 89
leadership, 31
learning, 10, 78
legislation, viii, 2, 3, 4, 6, 8, 30, 35, 45, 49, 51
lending, 47
licensing, 58, 89
likelihood, 37, 76
limitations, 38, 43
links, 37, 57, 58, 66, 90
loans, x, 29, 44, 47, 58, 78, 81, 82, 83, 89
local community, 45
local government, vii, viii, ix, x, 1, 2, 3, 6, 7, 8, 9, 10, 11, 12, 13, 14, 15, 16, 21, 27, 28, 29, 34, 35, 41, 44, 45, 47, 58, 63, 64, 82, 83, 85, 86, 87, 89
low-income, 11, 12, 18

M

maintenance, 12, 76, 77
management, 4, 8, 14, 15, 38, 58, 67, 74, 79, 85, 88, 89, 90
mandates, 8
manpower, 17
market value, 55
matching funds, 78
measurement, 14, 75
measures, 15, 45, 46, 63
media, 30, 84
Medicaid, 11, 19, 22
mentoring program, 42
military, 44
Minnesota, 80, 92
minority groups, 12
money, 9, 36, 41, 47, 50, 55, 64, 73, 84
mortality, 72

N

nation, 11, 84
National Endowment for the Arts (NEA), 54, 55, 87
National Endowment for the Humanities, 55, 87
National Institutes of Health, 80
Native American, 83
natural, 13
natural resources, 13
negotiation, 73
network, 57, 74
newsletters, 30, 35
nongovernmental organization, 8
non-profit, 44
nurses, 73

O

obligations, 49, 85
occupational, 13
Office of Justice Programs (OJP), 25, 55, 88
Office of Juvenile Justice and Delinquency Prevention, 42
Office of Management and Budget, 4, 23, 38, 43, 54, 58, 78, 79, 85, 88, 90
Office of Personnel Management, 49
overlap, viii, 2, 3, 15
oversight, 6, 9, 11, 17, 31, 35, 51

P

PART, 14, 15, 23

partnership, 79
peer review, 73
per capita, 12
personnel costs, 77
philanthropic, 56
philosophical, 72
philosophy, 30, 63
pilot study, 75
planning, x, 4, 10, 14, 21, 39, 47, 61, 63, 72
police, x, 28
policy makers, 11, 13
politicians, 9
poor, 12, 15, 71
population, 12, 14, 71, 72
pre-existing, 20
premiums, 47
preparedness, x, 28
President Nixon, 17, 23, 24
presidency, 15, 19
press, 30, 31, 33, 34, 35, 70
prevention, 21
prisoners, 42
private, vii, ix, x, xi, 13, 28, 29, 30, 32, 35, 36, 37, 38, 45, 47, 56, 57, 59, 61, 62, 63, 65, 66, 81, 82, 83, 90, 91
private firms, 47
private sector, 13
probation, 20
probation officers, 20
Program Assessment Rating Tool, 14, 23
progress reports, 36
project, vii, viii, x, 2, 3, 4, 5, 10, 31, 32, 33, 35, 37, 39, 40, 41, 43, 45, 47, 50, 56, 61, 63, 64, 66, 67, 68, 69, 70, 71, 72, 73, 74, 75, 76, 77, 78
property, 48, 55
public, vii, 1, 2, 9, 16, 17, 18, 32, 37, 49, 50, 55, 57, 58, 63, 64, 72, 84, 85
public health, vii, 1, 2, 17, 18
public sector, 32
public welfare, 16

Q

questionnaires, 14, 75

R

range, viii, 2, 3, 4, 5, 10, 14, 49
Reagan Administration, 12
real property, 48
recession, 42
recessions, 10
recipient discretion, viii, 2, 3, 4
recovery, ix, 28, 51, 52
regional, 8, 31, 34, 49, 52, 54, 55, 72, 79, 85, 86, 88
regulation, 8
regulations, 8, 35, 38, 49, 55, 58, 89
reimbursement, viii, 2, 3, 47
relationship, 9, 52
relationships, ix, 19, 27, 31, 75
Republican, 9
research and development, 14
resistance, 8
resources, vii, ix, x, xi, 11, 12, 13, 28, 30, 32, 39, 42, 56, 57, 58, 59, 61, 62, 65, 71, 73, 82, 88, 91
responsibilities, 30, 32, 49, 52
retirement, 77
returns, 56
revenue, viii, 2, 3, 4, 11, 17, 19, 22
risk, 21, 42, 56
rural, 17, 38, 65
rural development, 65

S

safety, 13
salaries, 77
salary, 77
sample, ix, 28, 33, 37, 39, 42, 67, 80, 89, 91, 92
savings, 18
SBA, 83
scholarships, 47, 59
school, 21, 29, 42, 82, 83
school performance, 42
search, ix, 28, 29, 34, 37, 43, 50, 51, 55, 57, 58, 66, 75, 82, 88

Index

searches, 72
searching, 32, 38, 40, 56, 85
secondary education, 18
security, x, 21, 28, 41, 44, 65, 90
selecting, 49
seminars, ix, 28, 38, 39, 90
September 11, 21
services, vii, 1, 2, 10, 13, 17, 18, 20, 22, 29, 44, 47, 49, 62, 64, 65, 66, 72, 73, 77, 82, 89
sharing, viii, 2, 3, 4, 10, 17, 19, 22
sign, xi, 51, 66, 81, 86
sites, x, 37, 39, 42, 62, 81, 89
skills, 71
Small Business Administration, 29, 55, 83, 88
Social Security, 16, 18, 23, 45
social services, vii, 1, 2, 7, 13, 18, 65
Social Services Block Grant, 7, 18
sponsor, ix, 28, 39, 56
staffing, 72, 73
stakeholders, 15
standards, 4, 20
State Council, 55, 87
State Grants, 52
State of the Union, 17
state office, ix, 27, 31, 37, 50, 52, 88
statistics, 71
statutes, 48
stimulus, ix, 28, 51, 53
strategic planning, 14
strategies, 34, 43, 56, 72
strength, 42
students, x, 29, 81
success rate, 30
summaries, 52
supervision, ix, 27, 30
supplements, x, 28, 55
supply, 35
support services, 21, 73

T

target populations, 9
taxes, 58, 88, 89

tax-exempt, 55, 65
technical assistance, 29, 47, 53, 83
Temporary Assistance for Needy Families, (TANF), vii, 1, 3, 5, 12, 19, 20, 23, 25
terrorism, x, 28
terrorist attack, 21
time frame, 72, 73, 75
title, x, 38, 68, 81
tracking, 33, 86
training, 12, 17, 19, 33, 35, 47, 56, 77, 90
transition, 21
transportation, 14, 17, 73, 77
treatment programs, 21
trust fund, 19

U

uniform, xi, 11, 50, 51, 81
United States, 8, 23, 43, 46, 52, 58, 89, 93
universities, 72

V

vandalism, 21
variation, viii, 2, 3, 43
veterans, 53, 82
victims, 21, 42
violence, 21
visible, 9
voting, 46

W

welfare, 12, 18
Wisconsin, 78
Workforce Investment Act, 7
workload, ix, 27, 30, 32
writing, vii, x, xi, 31, 32, 39, 41, 42, 61, 62, 63, 64, 67, 68, 73; 78, 80, 82, 85, 90, 92